SASHIKO
365

Stitch a new sashiko pattern
every day of the year

SUSAN BRISCOE

DAVID & CHARLES

www.davidandcharles.com

Introduction

The idea of a sashiko 'block' for every day of the year started with a challenge from my sashiko course students a few years ago. For many years, I've taught sashiko by stitching patterns on 4½in (11.5cm) squares, sewn together later into samplers – my friends in Yuza Sashiko Guild do this. Small squares are portable, sashiko can be stitched anywhere, and a big sashiko project is achievable if tackled in little pieces. My students learned different groups of patterns, drawing each onto their fabric, accenting sashiko with colour and growing their skills. But are there really enough different sashiko designs to stitch one every day for a year?

The answer is, 'Yes'! I started looking deeply into sashiko designs, discovering many pattern variations that I hadn't explored before. Some larger patterns yield more than one block with different parts of the design. The 365 blocks arrange neatly into a 19 x 19 block format, plus four 'cornerstone' blocks to create the Sashiko 365 quilt top, the ultimate sashiko sampler quilt, measuring a generous 96in (244cm) square finished. There's even an extra block provided – perfect for leap year stitching! – to make a quilt label. These blocks are also ideal for your own smaller projects, from coasters to cushions, as well as bags, table linen, wall hangings, and 'sew' on. Most of the patterns can be extended or repeated to create larger pieces of sashiko, too.

For my sample blocks, I chose a mid indigo blue and an easy to remember rainbow thread palette sequence, so you can see how the stitching lines progress and flow around each pattern. The blocks can be stitched in a more traditional white on dark indigo colourway, or in any colours you choose! Whether you stitch a block a day or tackle several at once is up to you, but as many people find, sashiko stitching every day can create a little oasis of calm.

Before turning to the pattern directory to begin your first block, do read through the Getting Started section, which gives all the information you need, from essential equipment to prepping materials, as well as outlining all the techniques, like marking fabric and sashiko stitching basics. Everything you need to know to turn your blocks into a stunning quilt is covered in Making the Quilt. I hope you enjoy your sashiko year!

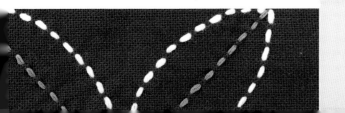

Getting Started

Different kinds of sashiko

There are three styles of sashiko designs: *hitomezashi* (one stitch sashiko), *moyōzashi* (pattern sashiko) and pictorial motifs. The first two are geometric and developed as a way to make farmers' and fishermen's clothing stronger and warmer in premodern Japan, particularly the north, mostly with white thread on indigo. Pictorial designs are rarer. Sashiko means 'little stab' or 'little pierce', for the stitching action.

 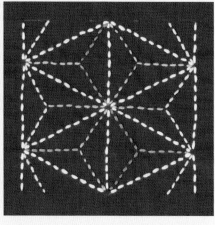 

Hitomezashi These designs look a little like blackwork. Mostly stitched on ¼in (6mm) grids, straight lines of running stitch go back and forth horizontally, vertically and sometimes diagonally. Stitches cross or meet to make the pattern and sometimes extra thread is woven through for *kugurizashi* ('go through' sashiko). The stitch length is dictated by the grid size, so usually ¼in (6mm) long, with the needle going up and down either on the grid crosses or in the squares.

Moyouzashi Grids are marked in various sizes for larger patterns where the stitch lines bend, curve or cross. The stitch length is around ⅛in (3mm) and the gap between stitches about ¹⁄₁₆in (1.5mm), although this varies a little to fit the stitches to the pattern repeat. Stitches don't cross on the front of the work, only on the back, with a tiny gap on the front where lines cross. The more lines, the bigger this gap must be. Stitches are not counted, but note how many are in shorter sections of the pattern, and maintain that number throughout. The order of stitching the lines is adapted for the smaller square size so always follow the instructions for each block.

Pictorial motifs These include seasonal leaves and flowers, kanji characters, and *kamon* (Japanese family crests). Patterns are traced directly off the pattern directory page onto the fabric squares. There are no set rules for stitching these, so I've given some basic tips as to order of stitching for ease of working. But by the time you get to these, you'll be a sashiko stitching expert!

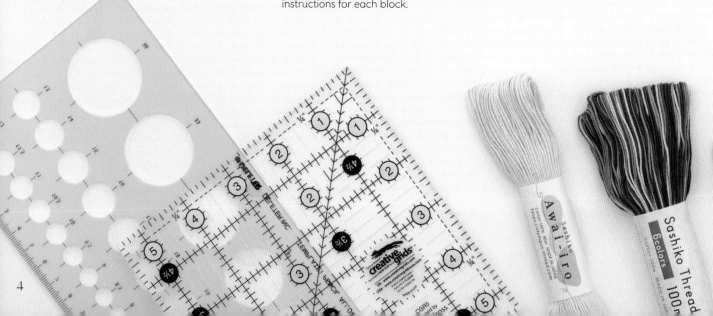

Tools and Materials

This section outlines all the things you will need to stitch the sashiko blocks featured in this book, and the chances are you'll have most of what you require already. Sashiko equipment, threads and fabrics are widely available by mail order online (see Suppliers) but substitutions can be made. For additional requirements for making your blocks into a quilt, please refer to Making the Quilt.

Marking equipment

The majority of the block patterns in this book were marked directly onto the fabric using a marking pen, an ordinary ruler and one of the marking grids supplied (see Marking Grids); some need circle templates of various sizes and, for a few of the patterns, a set square or protractor is required. For the blocks with pictorial designs, a lightbox was used to trace the motif onto the fabric, although you can improvise by using a window.

MARKING PEN OR PENCIL

I marked all my blocks using a white marking pen (fine) from Clover, a refillable ball pen with waxy 'ink' that can be ironed off or washed out. Other suitable options include propelling pencils for use on fabric with white or light yellow leads; white or light quilter's marking pencils; or white artist's watercolour pencils. Your aim is to make a fine line that shows up well on your fabric and that stays on while you stitch, but that is easy to remove once stitching is complete. Frixion pens are not recommended as they can bleach some solid dyed fabrics.

CUTTING MAT AND QUILTER'S RULER

These are excellent for the precision marking and cutting out (when used with a rotary cutter) of your 4½in (11.5cm) fabric squares. An A3 or A2 size mat and a ruler that is 24in (60cm) long and at least 4½in (11.5cm) wide is best. The lines on the mat will also be handy for drawing the pattern grids onto your fabric squares. (It is possible, of course, to cut 365 squares by hand, but you will need an accurate 4½in (11.5cm) square template to draw around and a good pair of fabric scissors.)

RULER, COMPASS, PROTRACTOR AND SET SQUARE

An ordinary 6in (15cm) or 12in (30cm) ruler is best when marking the sashiko grids onto your cut out fabric squares (do not use a quilter's ruler as it is designed to grip and can drag the fabric as you mark). A compass enables you to make circle templates of any size and you can draw 60° (isometric) angles using a protractor or set squares. In fact, you will find that an inexpensive school geometry set has everything you require.

CIRCLE TEMPLATES AND STENCILS

Use your compass (or a circle cutter) to cut the following circle sizes from scraps of clear, thin plastic packaging or recycled card. Metric sizes are not always exact equivalents to imperial, but work just as well.

IMPERIAL	METRIC
⅝in	1.5cm
¾in	2cm
1in	2.5cm
1⅛in	3cm
1½in	4cm
2in	5cm
2⅜in	6cm
2½in	6.5cm
2¾in	7cm
3in	8cm
3½in	9cm
4½in	11.5cm
5in	12.5cm

Sewing equipment

EMBROIDERY SCISSORS OR SNIPS

Using *nigiri basami* (traditional Japanese embroidery snips) to cut threads makes stitching sashiko feel very authentic, but a pair of small embroidery scissors is fine.

SASHIKO NEEDLES

Sashiko needles are very sharp, strong, and don't bend in use. You need at least one long and one short needle: a long needle is good for patterns with straight lines; a shorter needle is better for changing direction often. Because I used coloured threads for my blocks, I used seven needles, one for each thread colour, to save rethreading. If you can't find sashiko needles, try embroidery crewels instead.

THIMBLE

Thimbles are optional – I don't use one. If you like to use a thimble, then do. Traditional Japanese *yubinuki* thimbles are made from leather or metal, or embroidered with silk. A ring thimble **(A)** is worn on the second joint of the middle finger of the sewing hand so the eye end of the needle rests against it. The coin thimble **(B)**, worn at the base of your finger, has a dimpled disk to push the needle through.

Sashiko thread

The sashiko blocks are designed to be stitched with either fine 4-ply sashiko thread doubled (what I used), or medium 6-ply sashiko thread used singly (this is more widely available). Old sashiko usually has the finer thread used doubled, making the stitches very bold. Sashiko thread is a strong, matte cotton thread. Most modern sashiko threads are mercerised (passed through a gas flame at high speed to burn off any fluff). If sashiko thread is unavailable, no.12 coton à broder or perlé doubled, or single no.8 perlé are good alternatives, although perlé is shiny, not matte. Thread comes in skeins, and on cards and cones.

I used coloured threads for my block samples to guide you through stitching each block (see Using the Pattern Directory), following the order of colours in the pastel rainbow – pink, peach, yellow, green, blue and lilac. You can choose your own colours, or just one colour. Traditionally sashiko stitching was white thread on blue fabric, but today sashiko threads are available in many colours, so you can coordinate your finished project with your own décor. If using multiple colours, using one needle per colour saves rethreading, maximising thread use.

HOW MUCH THREAD DO I NEED?

The table gives approximate amounts of sashiko threads based on what I used to stitch my blocks, given in popular skein and card sizes. If you choose to stitch using just a single colour, you will need eight 170m skeins for 4-ply doubled or eight 100m skeins for 6-ply used singly.

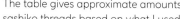

PREPARING SASHIKO THREAD FOR USE

Sashiko thread is mostly sold in skeins, wound and tied like knitting yarn and, unlike stranded cotton (floss) embroidery thread, the threads don't pull out from the skein. First open out the skein, removing the paper band. Look for the extra loop of thread tied around the skein and cut through all the threads at this point **(C)**. The threads will be very long but don't cut them! Hold the loop end of the skein and loosely plait the threads to keep them tidy **(D)**. It is a good idea to thread the skein band back on before you plait. Draw out individual threads as you need them from the top of the plait. The thread is a good length to use doubled, but cut 6-ply medium thread in half to use singly.

A

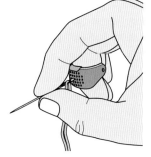

B

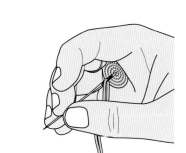

4-PLY FINE (DOUBLED)	6-PLY MEDIUM (SINGLE)
white 170m x 3	white 100m x 3
pink 170m x 2	pink 100m x 2
peach 170 x 1	peach 100m x 1
yellow 40m x 3	yellow 100m x 1
green 170m x 1	green 100m x 1
blue 170m x 1	blue 100m x 1
lilac 40m x 3	lilac 100m x 1

C

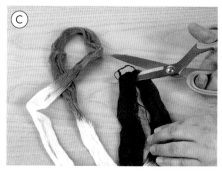

D

Fabric for blocks

I used a colourfast mid-indigo 100% cotton fabric specially woven for sashiko by Olympus Thread Mfg Co., Japan (also available in cream and dark indigo). Cotton fabric for sashiko has a lower thread count (number of threads per inch or centimetre) than patchwork cotton, so stitching is easier with the thicker sashiko thread. Many homespun-style patchwork cottons can substitute, or dressmaking linen and cotton blends. You can use any colour – it doesn't have to be blue – but buy the fabric in one piece to make sure of the same dye lot.

BLOCK FABRIC REQUIREMENTS

To stitch the blocks the fabric quantity required will depend on the fabric width chosen (note: for extra fabrics to make the sampler quilt top, see Making the Quilt).

+ For 42–44in (107–110cm) wide fabric – 5¼yd (4.8m)

+ For 56in (142cm) wide fabric – 4yd (3.6m)

+ For 14½in (37cm) wide fabric (traditional Japanese narrow width) – 15½yd (14.2m)

Check chosen fabric for shrinkage by spritzing lightly with water and ironing dry. If it shrinks, preshrink the whole bolt the same way, or wash, starch and iron it.

PREPARING THE FABRIC SQUARES

Once you have made your fabric selection, it is time to prepare the squares. It is important to zigzag or faux overlock the edges of each square before you start your sashiko stitching to stop them fraying. Use a stitch narrower than the ¼in (6mm) seam allowance, so the edge stitching disappears into the seam allowance when the blocks are sewn together. Follow the method described in the steps below to edge a few dozen strips at a time. It is slightly quicker than sewing around the squares individually and prevents their corners from scrunching up. Choose contrasting threads so you can see at a glance if a fabric square is the right way up.

1. Cut fabric into 4½in (11.5cm) strips. Wider fabric may be folded on the bolt and you can leave it folded while you cut, ensuring your ruler is at right angles to the fold, so that the strip doesn't kink in the middle (it also shows the front and back of the fabric).

+ 42–44in (107–110cm) wide fabric – cut 41 strips

+ 56in (142cm) wide fabric – cut 31 strips

+ 14½in (37cm) wide fabric – cut 123 strips

If rotary cutting, cut with the measurements on the ruler, not the mat, for accuracy.

2. Select a zigzag or faux overlock stitch on your sewing machine (I used a stretch overlock stitch on my Bernina) and use two distinctly different shades of thread for the top and the bobbin threads (I used bright green on top, with sage green in the bobbin). Zigzag or faux overlock all the way down each of the the long edges on each strip: these will become the top and bottom edges of each square **(E)**.

3. Now cut each strip into 4½in (11.5cm) squares, keeping your ruler at a right angle to the long edge, so your squares are truly square. You may need to trim a skinny wedge off the short edge occasionally to keep cutting at 90°. Pressing to remove the centre fold if there is one, cut:

+ From 42–44in (107–110cm) strips – 9 squares

+ From 56in (142cm) strips – 12 squares

+ From 14½in (37cm) strips – 3 squares

This time using the same colour thread for both top *and* bobbin threads (I used sage green), zigzag or faux overlock along the other two raw edges on each square: these are the sides. Chain piecing the edging as shown, leaving almost no thread between the squares, saves a lot of thread **(F)**. Store your squares flat in a box or bag till needed.

Some blocks, like pattern 79, have a very obvious right way up, but some can accidentally be turned on their side. By using a different top thread colour for the edging stitch for the top and bottom, this should never be a problem. If you were to turn this square over the edging stitch all the way around would match the colour of the edging stitch on sides on the front of the square. You could also draw a small arrow on the back of the block for an extra reminder.

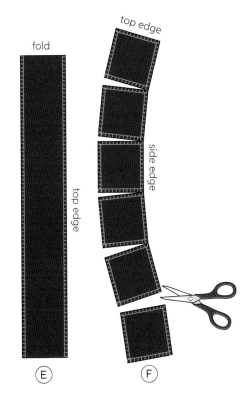

Techniques

This section covers the basics of marking the patterns onto your fabric squares, as well as advice on how to stitch sashiko, although the specific details of stitching each block are given in the pattern directory. Mark each block pattern as needed or in small batches, rather than all in one go. Once some are marked, you can start stitching.

Marking the grids

The easiest way to mark a grid is to put the fabric square onto a gridded background and use a ruler, or any straight edge, to draw lines across the square, linking up the lines from the grid behind. A small cutting mat, only slightly larger than the fabric, is ideal for this, but I have created two mark up grids to make this even easier (see Mark Up Grids). Please take a look at these now. You can use these to mark your patterns in exactly the same way as the lines on a cutting mat following the step instructions.

PICTORIAL MOTIFS

Blocks 348–365 are pictorial motifs. Photocopy or trace the motifs directly from the pattern directory, darkening the lines with a fairly thick black pen. Fold the fabric square in quarters to locate the centre. Match the centre of the fabric square to the centre of the template and pin in place. Position against your light source, either a light box or a window (but choose a sunny day), then simply trace the pattern lines through the fabric. The template will show through even the darkest fabric when strongly lit.

THE BASIC MARKING METHOD

1. Each block instruction includes the spacing of the grid lines and the number of squares or rectangles in the grid, e.g. 'Mark ½in (1.3cm) grid, 6 x 6 squares'. Mark the centre of each side of your fabric square by folding it in half at the edge, then place it on the appropriate grid pattern, lining up the centre folds of the square with the centre of the grid lines (marked with an arrow). Drawing the lines vertically, use a ruler to link the lines on either side of the square and your chosen fabric marker to draw the lines right out to the edge – if the fabric slips, you can easily realign it. Depending on the marker you are using, you may need to allow a few seconds for the 'ink' to dry after drawing each line (as is the case with the white marking pen (fine) from Clover) for the white line to appear **(A)**.

2. It is easiest to always draw the lines vertically, as the line you are drawing can be clearly seen at the side of the ruler. So simply rotate the fabric square through 90° to draw the second set of grid lines **(B)**.

3. Where the pattern structure is divided by three, a ½in (1.3mm) grid pattern is often used, as in the instruction 'Mark ½in (1.3cm) grid, 6 x 6 squares' **(C)**.

4. Where the pattern structure divides best by four, the ⅜in (1cm) grid pattern is used, as in the instruction 'Mark ⅜in (1cm) grid, 8 x 8 squares' **(D)**. (A few patterns need 1⁄16in (1.5mm) measurements and for these you should draw between the ⅛in (3mm) markings.)

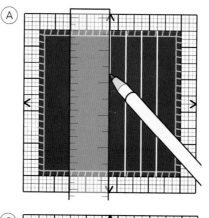

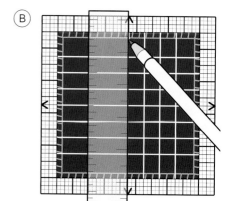

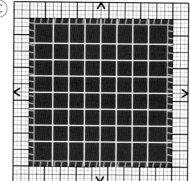

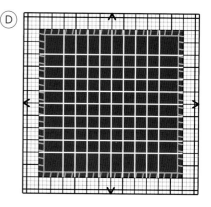

MARKING VARIATIONS

After the grid is drawn, the rest of the pattern can be marked with the fabric on any surface. Here are a few examples to illustrate the variations on the grid patterns for the drawing of the geometric blocks. Note: patterns 1–347 are geometric blocks.

Many patterns require additional diagonal lines, such as pattern 217. Draw these as described in the pattern instructions **(E)**.

Patterns marked on rectangular grids, rather than square ones, like pattern 295, may be more easily drawn by using one grid after the other, e.g. ½in x ⅜in (1.3cm x 1cm) **(F)**.

Some patterns have more complex diagonal lines, like pattern 318, where the diagonal lines link corners across several rectangles or squares rather than from corner to corner in just one **(G)**.

Circles or curves are added for some patterns. like pattern 32, so circle template sizes are included in the pattern instructions. Line up a circle with the grid as shown in the block diagram **(H)**.

A few patterns have 60° angles (patterns 238, 279 and 346) and one has 72° angles (pattern 107). Use a protractor to mark these angles, or a hexagon template, or a 60/30 set square to mark 60° and a pentagon to mark 72° **(I)**.

Sashiko stitching

STARTING AND FINISHING

For very secure stitching, start and finish with a knot. Thread your needle with approx. 1yd (1m) sashiko thread (one length from the skein) if you are doubling the thread, or half that for threads used singly. Smooth the thread down to remove excess twist (this is especially important if you are using a doubled thread) – try holding the thread taut and snapping it with your thumbs, too. Tie a double knot in the end **(J)**. Begin stitching with the knot on the back of your work. To finish, again tie a knot on the back: hold the needle against the back of the last stitch, wrap the thread around it several times, then holding the knot against the fabric with your thumb, pull the needle through **(K)**. The knots will not be seen from the front.

E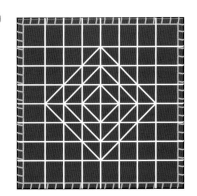

F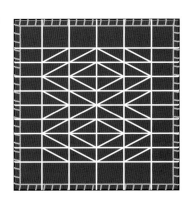

G

H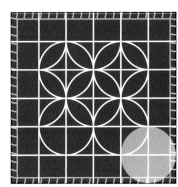

I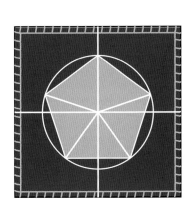

J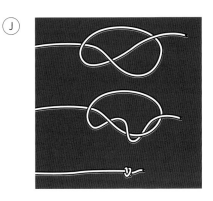

K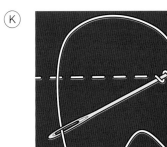

STITCHING ACTION

Traditionally, running stitch in Japan is sewn using a technique called *unshin*, which means 'moving needle', although it is the fabric that moves rather than the needle! The fabric is pleated onto the needle tip with an up-and-down motion **(L)**; the needle is held quite still. Once several stitches are loaded onto the needle, the fabric is pulled off the back of the needle (rather than trying to push the needle through), with the fabric slightly gathered up by the thread. This is then eased out in a step called *itokoki* or 'thread exhalation' by pushing the fabric along the thread, rather like pulling out curtain gathers. This stitching motion is essential if you are using a doubled thread, to ensure the two strands lie parallel to each other in the stitch rather than becoming twisted.

Stitch sashiko lines side to side, holding the fabric square in your hand **(M)**. No hoop or frame is necessary (the blocks would be too small for these anyway). Where there is a very sharp change of direction, such as on a *hitomezashi* design, leave a small turning loop of thread on the back (see Sashiko Stitching Tips).

MAKING A HATAMUSUBI (LOOM KNOT)

Learning how to tie a *hatamusubi* (loom knot) will will make the most of your sashiko thread, down to the last ½in (1.3cm). It's especially useful for *hitomezashi* (one stitch sashiko) designs where a lot of thread is used. The harder the knot is pulled, the tighter it becomes. Moisten the ends of the threads to make it easier to tie. The secret is the way the short ends of the thread are held whilst the knot is tied. Instructions are the same for right- and left-handed stitchers as both hands do equal work!

1. Leave a 1in (2.5cm) tail of old thread loose on the back of work (shown in white). Thread the needle but do not knot the new thread. Lay the end(s) of the new thread (shown in red) against the back of the work.

2. Hold the end of the new thread between the first two fingers of your left hand (at point A). Use your left thumb to bend the tail of the old thread over the new. Put your thumb on the crossed threads to hold them. Keep holding these two points until instructed otherwise.

3. Now the long part of the new thread does most of the work. Loop it to the left, as shown by the arrow. Lift your thumb quickly, pass the thread under it and hold the crossed threads firmly again.

4. Take the long part of the new thread under its own tail and over the old thread. At this point you will see that the new thread has made a loop.

5. Continue to hold the thread at point A. Use your right index finger to bend the old thread through the loop and hold the end between your left thumb and left ring finger at point B. Holding the two short ends so they can't flip out of the knot, use the long new thread to gently pull the knot closed with your right hand, as shown by the arrow.

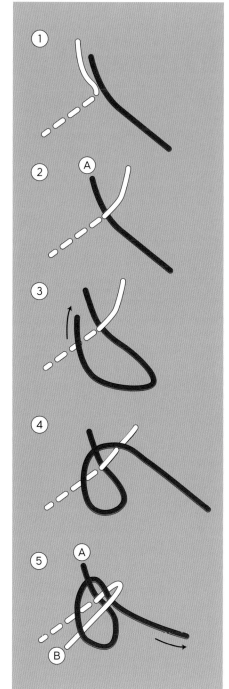

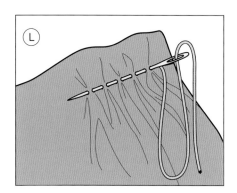

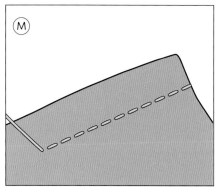

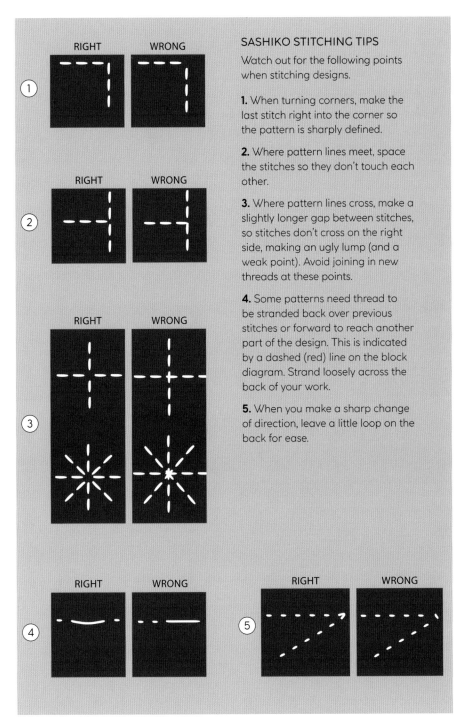

SASHIKO STITCHING TIPS

Watch out for the following points when stitching designs.

1. When turning corners, make the last stitch right into the corner so the pattern is sharply defined.

2. Where pattern lines meet, space the stitches so they don't touch each other.

3. Where pattern lines cross, make a slightly longer gap between stitches, so stitches don't cross on the right side, making an ugly lump (and a weak point). Avoid joining in new threads at these points.

4. Some patterns need thread to be stranded back over previous stitches or forward to reach another part of the design. This is indicated by a dashed (red) line on the block diagram. Strand loosely across the back of your work.

5. When you make a sharp change of direction, leave a little loop on the back for ease.

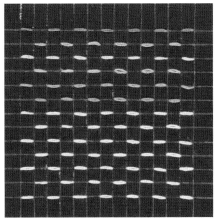

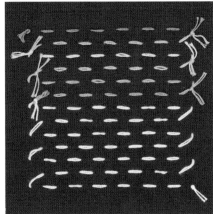

WARM UP STITCHING EXERCISE

Let's warm up by stitching this simple *hitomezashi* (one stitch sashiko) pattern, basic *yokogushi* (horizontal rows), which is turned on its side and stitched vertically for the foundation for patterns 1–18, but used horizontally (with the addition of an extra row!) for patterns 180–185.

Mark ¼in (6mm) grid, 12 x 13 squares. Stitch horizontal lines back and forth, starting from the top down. Leave a generous turning loop at the end of each row. Join in each change of colour or new thread with a *hatamusubi* knot, which can be used anywhere in the design.

This sample isn't one of your 365 blocks, so don't worry too much about any mistakes, but do try to stitch accurately and maintain an even tension, practising those turning loops at the ends of the rows.

And now, your sashiko year awaits . . .

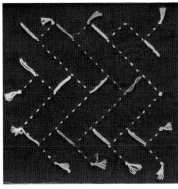

Sashiko does not look identical on the front and back as shown here on pattern 229. Turn it to the back and you can see the starting and finishing knots, and how the thread is stranded to go from one part of the design to the next.

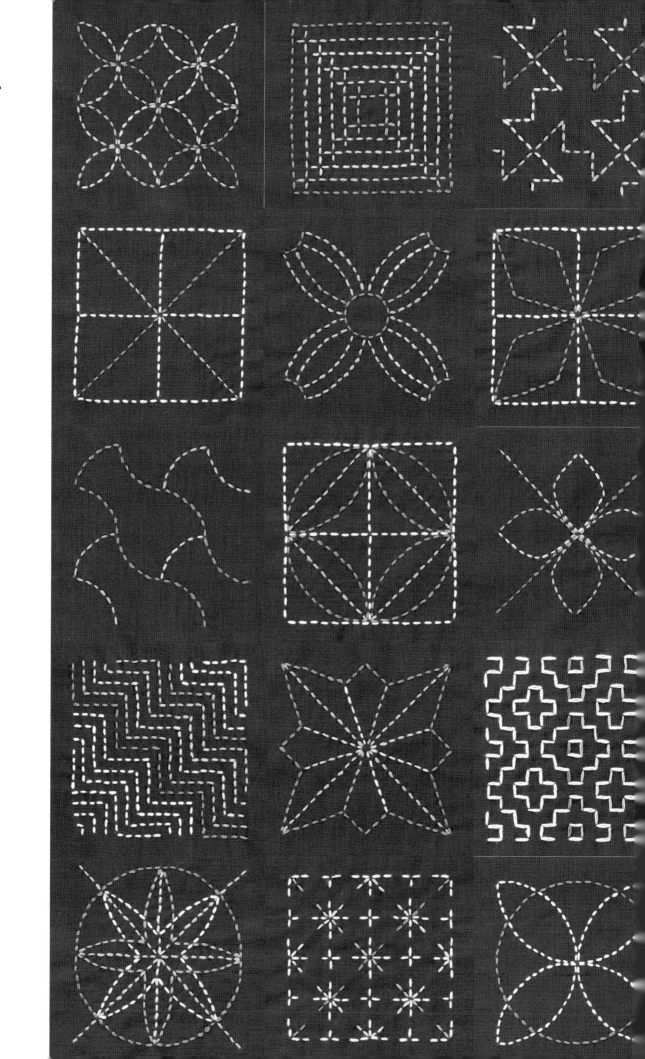

Pattern Directory

Using the Pattern Directory

1. Blocks are grouped together with similar designs, and colour bands on the page indicate these groupings across pages.

2. Each block is numbered and they have been arranged to be stitched in number sequence, to enable you to build your sashiko skills as you mark and stitch.

3. Each block name is given in Japanese and English. Some blocks share a name, because more than one block was made by focusing on different areas of the larger pattern. Some patterns are completely different, yet have the same name, while some have multiple names in Japanese – I've chosen just one name for the pattern directory.

4. The pattern type of each block is indicated by letters after the block number (see Pattern Type Key).

5. The foundation grid drawn on the fabric is indicated on the pattern diagram in light blue with actual stitch lines in black.

6. Red arrows indicate stitching direction, with stranding across the back of the fabric, if applicable, shown as a dashed line.

7. The block diagrams are complemented with the finished block sample photo, stitched in a rainbow order using a pastel palette (pink, peach, yellow, green, blue, lilac). Follow the colours *and* the arrows.

8. The foundation grid measurements including the numbers of units in the grid are noted in the text, height first, width second, e.g., 'Mark ¼in (6mm) grid, 12 x 13 squares'.

9. Stitching instructions may refer back to another block, if a pattern is made with additional stitch lines on top of a previous design, but colour information relates to the block on the page.

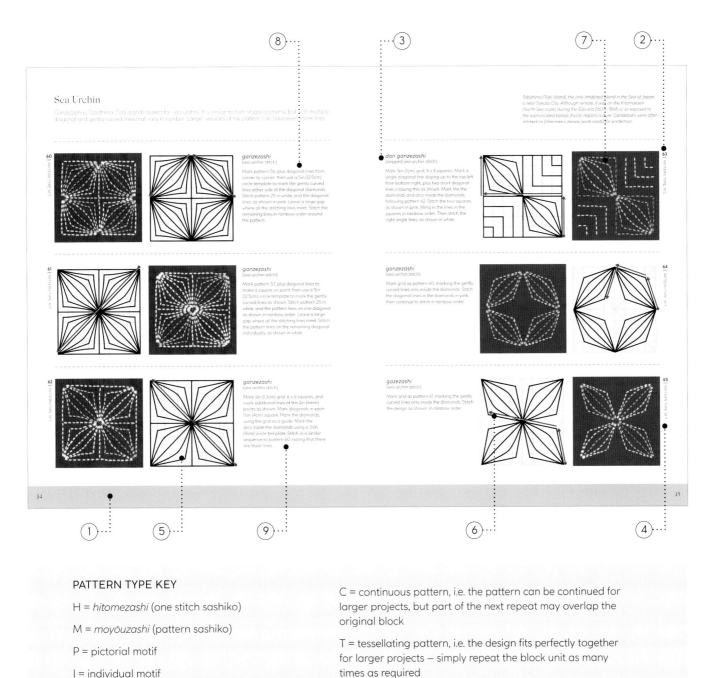

PATTERN TYPE KEY

H = *hitomezashi* (one stitch sashiko)

M = *moyōuzashi* (pattern sashiko)

P = pictorial motif

I = individual motif

C = continuous pattern, i.e. the pattern can be continued for larger projects, but part of the next repeat may overlap the original block

T = tessellating pattern, i.e. the design fits perfectly together for larger projects – simply repeat the block unit as many times as required

Weaves and Crosses

All of these patterns share a common foundation, the basic *yokogushi* (horizontal rows) pattern. By weaving through the stitches with a single thread for contrast, we make *kugurizashi* ('go through' sashiko).

1 | PATTERN TYPE: H C

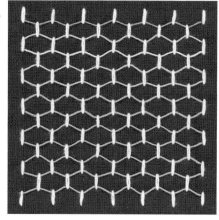

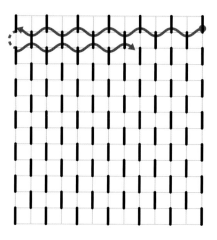

kikkōzashi
(hexagon stitch)

Mark ¼in (6mm) grid, 13 x 12 squares. Stitch *yokogushi* (see Techniques: Warm Up Stitching Exercise) as vertical lines. Weave in and out of the stitches, starting under the first stitch, in rainbow order. Use the eye end of the needle to thread through, not the point, so you don't pierce stitches accidentally. Take a small stitch to the back at the end of each row.

2 | PATTERN TYPE: H C

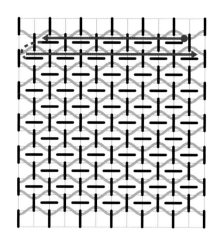

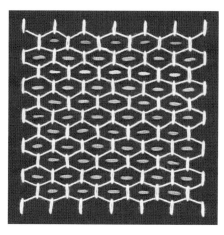

kawari kikkōzashi
(hexagon stitch variation)

Mark and stitch pattern 1 in white. Stitch horizontal running stitch rows in rainbow order. Note: the running stitch rows may be worked after each woven row, if preferred, using the same thread.

3 | PATTERN TYPE: H C

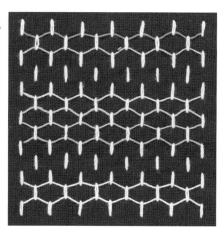

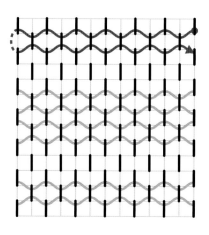

kawari kikkōzashi
(hexagon stitch variation)

Mark and stitch pattern 1, omitting the third, fourth, ninth and tenth woven rows.

Hexagon patterns, named after the turtle's shell, a creature said to live for 10,000 years, represent a wish for a long life. Kogin (counted sashiko) was sometimes edged with these stitches. The Japanese kanji character for '10' is a cross, so lots of crosses represent a wish for wealth or prosperity.

fukumame
(lucky beans)

Mark ¼in (6mm) grid, 13 x 13 squares. Stitch pattern 204. Weave in and out of each pair of stitches, as for pattern 1. Stitch horizontal rows as pattern 2. A shaded or multicoloured thread looks very effective for the horizontal running stitches.

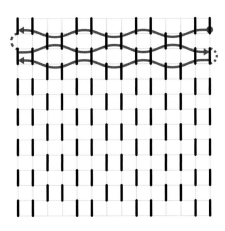
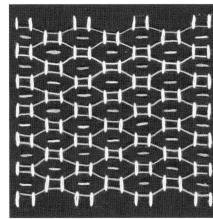

jūjizashi
('10' cross stitch)

Mark ¼in (6mm) grid, 13 x 12 squares. Stitch *yokogushi* (see Techniques: Warm Up Stitching Exercise) as vertical lines. A second set of stitches cross over the first at right angles, connecting the centres of the grid squares, worked in rainbow order and continuing in white.

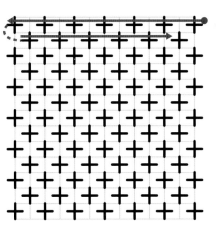

jūjihishikaha
(woven cross diamond)

Mark pattern 5. Stitch in white, horizontal rows first, then vertical columns, odd numbers only (first, third, fifth, etc.), so the vertical stitches cross the horizontal ones. Weave in and out of the stitches in rainbow order (note: the lower part of the pattern was woven with a multicoloured thread). The woven threads cross behind the running stitches.

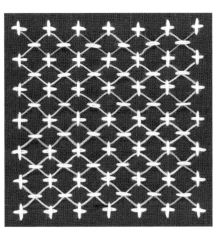

Rice Stitches

Combining diagonal stitches with the *jūjizashi* ('10' cross stitch) gives a variety of patterns named after the kanji character for rice – a cross with four diagonals. The first four patterns use a single diagonal thread.

 *The kanji character for rice*

---

7 | PATTERN TYPE: H C

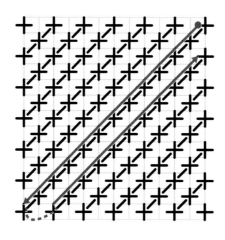

han komezashi
(half rice stitch)

Mark and stitch pattern 5 in white. Stitch rows of diagonal stitches in rainbow order, taking a tiny stitch behind the intersection of each cross and keeping the diagonals straight. Note: diagonals look good in a contrasting thread colour or thickness.

---

8 | PATTERN TYPE: H C

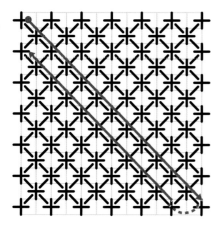

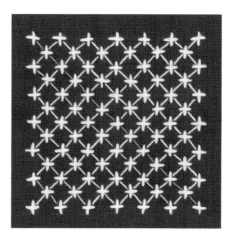

komezashi
(rice stitch)

Mark and stitch pattern 7 in white. Stitch a second set of diagonal lines, leaning in the opposite direction in rainbow order, to complete *komezashi*.

---

9 | PATTERN TYPE: H C

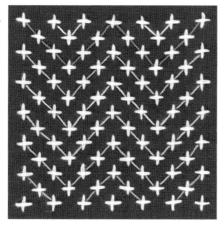

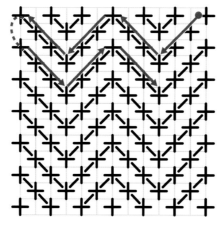

kawari komezashi
(rice stitch variation)

Mark and stitch pattern 5 in white. Stitch diagonal lines to form a zigzag pattern, in rainbow order.

The many variations on rice stitch can be combined together easily on larger pieces, since they all share the same foundation of crosses. The most elaborate rice stitch 'samplers' were fishermen's jackets from Awaji Island, near Kobe, which were covered top to bottom with rice stitch variations.

kawari komezashi
(rice stitch variation)

Mark and stitch pattern 5. Stitch diagonally in two directions, as shown, but skip every other diagonal line, to create crosses within diamond squares.

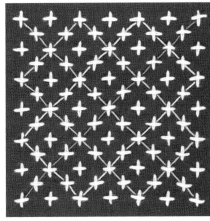

10

PATTERN TYPE: H C

kawari komezashi
(rice stitch variation)

Mark and stitch pattern 5. Stitch diagonally between the crosses in both directions, in rainbow order. Keep diagonal lines straight.

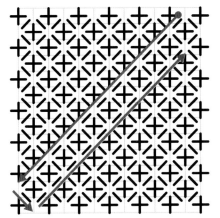

11

PATTERN TYPE: H C

kawari komezashi
(rice stitch variation)

Mark and stitch pattern 5. Stitch diagonally between the crosses, but skip every other diagonal line to create a square on point variation.

12

PATTERN TYPE: H C

17

More Rice Stitch Variations

Komezashi (rice stitch) can be arranged into borders, while the ends of *jūjizashi* ('10' cross stitch) can be linked with diagonal stitches for more patterns. The first two patterns use a single diagonal thread.

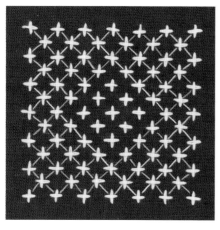

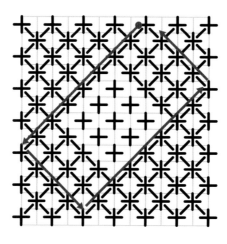

komezashi haichi
(rice stitch arrangement)

Mark and stitch pattern 5. Stitch pattern 12, but leave part of the diagonal lines unstitched to make a central square on point with crosses. Stitch most of the diagonals as a series of overlapping rectangles, as shown in pink, peach and yellow, and complete the four corners individually.

komezashi haichi
(rice stitch arrangement)

Mark and stitch pattern 5. Stitch pattern 12, but stitch the diagonal lines in the centre only to make a square on point. Outline the square in pink, then infill with diagonal lines in rainbow order, stitching back and forth.

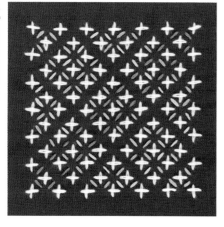

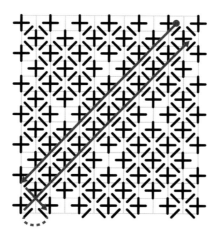

kawari komezashi
(rice stitch variation)

Mark and stitch pattern 5 in white. Stitch diagonally between the crosses, starting with the pink rows and continuing in rainbow order, skipping every third diagonal line to create a series of squares on point.

The kawari jūjitsunagi *(linked '10 cross' variations) were inspired by a very old sashiko fragment from Akita Prefecture. Presumably once part of a* noragi *(work jacket), it plays with variations on the basic pattern by changing the frequency and placement of the diagonal lines.*

jūjitsunagi
(linked '10' cross)

Mark and stitch pattern 5. Stitch diagonally to link the ends of the crosses, omitting alternate diagonal rows of crosses. Keep the diagonal lines straight.

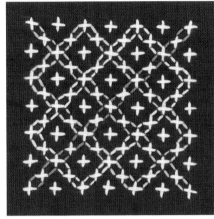

16 ‖ PATTERN TYPE: H C

kawari jūnitsunagi
(linked '10' cross variation)

Mark and stitch pattern 5. Stitch diagonally around the pattern in rainbow order, leaving the central crosses unlinked.

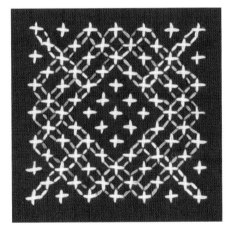
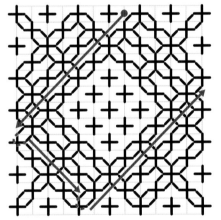

17 ‖ PATTERN TYPE: H C

kawari jūnitsunagi
(linked '10' cross variation)

Mark and stitch pattern 5. Stitch diagonally from top right to bottom left across the pattern in rainbow order. Repeat to stitch diagonally from top left to bottom right.

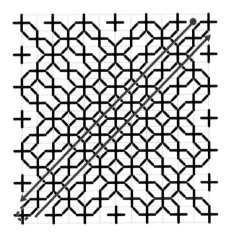
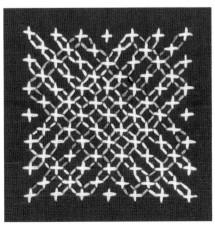

18 ‖ PATTERN TYPE: H I

19

Simple Grids

Basic grids are patterns in their own right as well as the foundation for other designs. Add diagonal lines and omit some stitches for *hanazashi* (flower stitch) patterns, which are like larger versions of *komezashi* (rice stitch).

 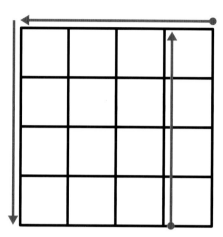

koshi
(check)

Mark ¾in (2cm) grid, 4 x 4 squares. Stitch the outer square in white, and stitch vertical lines, then horizontal lines in rainbow order.

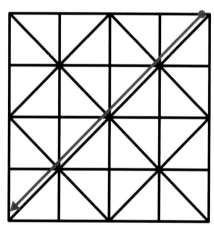 

taikakusen
(diagonal lines)

Mark pattern 19. Mark diagonal pattern lines as shown. Stitch pattern 19. Stitch diagonal lines, first pink and then peach. Then stitch remaining diagonal lines as shown in yellow.

  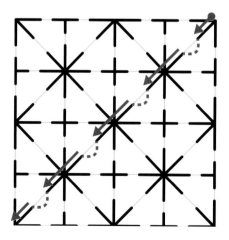

hanazashi
(flower stitch)

Mark pattern 20 and stitch in the same sequence, but omitting some stitches: stitch two stitches before and after each diagonal cross point, and one stitch before and after each cross point on the outer square.

Patterns like these may seem incredibly simple, and indeed they are! While they were often used for sashiko stitched through many layers, to make rugs for example, they also appear as a foil to more elaborate patterns on noragi (work jackets). Hanazashi (flower stitch) patterns look great stitched on checked fabrics.

niiju taikakusen
(doubled diagonal lines)

Mark pattern 20. Mark a second set of diagonal pattern lines as shown. Stitch as pattern 20, then stitch the second set of diagonal lines in green and blue.

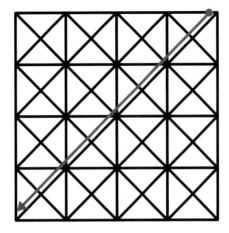

hanazashi
(flower stitch)

Mark and stitch pattern 21, but this time stitch just one stitch before and after each line crosses another.

koshi
(check)

Mark ½in (1.3cm) grid, 6 x 6 squares. Stitch the outer square in white, then stitch the vertical lines first, then the horizontal lines, in rainbow order.

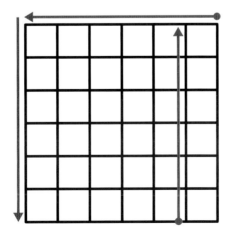
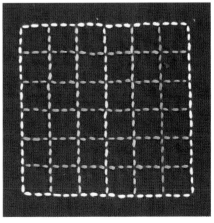

Large Grids

These are used as the foundations for many more complex patterns and are also stitched as a simple foil to more elaborate sashiko designs on larger pieces. They are some of the easiest patterns to mark.

koshi
(check)

Mark 1½in (4cm) grid, 2 x 2 squares. Stitch the outer square in pink, then stitch the lines across the centre in peach and yellow.

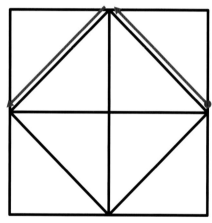

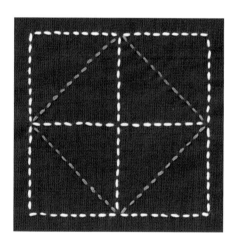

taikakusen
(diagonal lines)

Mark pattern 25. Mark diagonal pattern lines as shown to make a square on point. Stitch the grid lines as pattern 25 in white, then stitch the diagonal lines in pink.

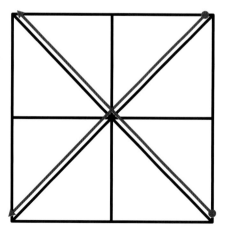

taikakusen
(diagonal lines)

Mark pattern 25 and mark diagonal lines from corner to corner. Stitch the grid lines as pattern 25 in white, then stitch the diagonal lines, pink then peach.

taikakusen
(diagonal lines)

Mark pattern 26, then mark additional diagonal lines as pattern 27. Stitch pattern 27 in white, then stitch the square on point (as pattern 26) in pink.

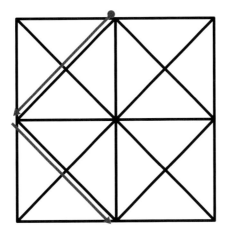
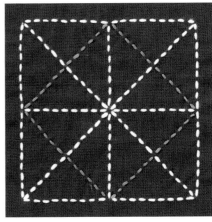

taikakusen
(diagonal lines)

Mark pattern 25, and mark additional diagonal lines slanting in one direction only. Stitch the grid lines as pattern 25 in white, then stitch diagonal lines individually in pink, peach and yellow.

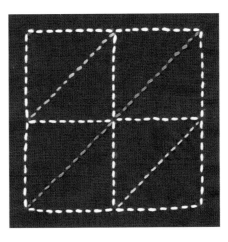
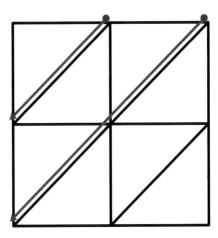

taikakusen
(diagonal lines)

Mark pattern 28. Leaving the outer square unstitched, stitch the inner square on point, as shown in pink, and the diagonal lines peach and yellow.

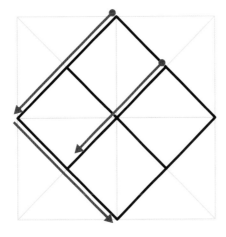

Circles and Layered Circles

Circles can be layered up to create many sashiko patterns. Use grids plus different sized circle templates to mark many variations on traditional designs, stitching circles in continuous wavy lines rather than individually.

31

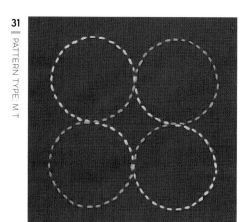 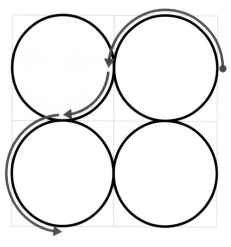

maru tsunagi
(linked circles)

Mark 1½in (4cm) grid, 2 x 2 squares. Use a 1½in (4cm) circle template to mark the pattern, lining up the circles with the squares. Stitch in continuous wavy lines (not individual circles) in pink and peach.

32

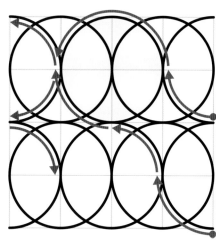 

kasane maru tsunagi
(layered linked circles)

Mark ¾in (2cm) grid, 4 x 4 squares. Mark pattern 31. Use a 1½in (4cm) circle template to mark overlapping circles. Stitch pattern 31 in white, and then stitch continuous wavy lines (not individual circles) in pink, peach and yellow.

33

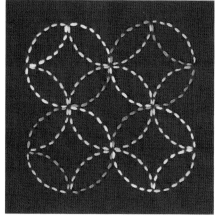 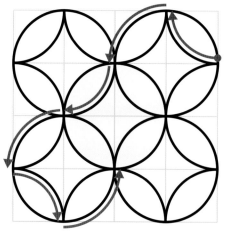

shippō tsunagi
(linked seven treasures)

Mark ¾in (2cm) grid, 4 x 4 squares. Mark patttern 31. Draw overlapping circles using a 1½in (4cm) circle template, and then stitch continuous wavy lines (not individual circles) in rainbow order.

Shippō *(seven treasures)* was originally, more descriptively, called wachigai *(layered circles)*. The 'seven treasures' are symbolic of Buddhist virtues – gold, silver, lapis lazuli, agate, seashell, amber and coral. It may be a pun on 'shiho' *('four steps' or 'four directions')*. My sashiko students 'invented' pattern 32 by mistake!

shippō tsunagi
(linked seven treasures)

Mark ¾in (2cm) grid, 4 x 4 squares. Draw overlapping circles using a 1½in (4cm) circle template. Stitch peach and pink wavy lines, then complete in rainbow order.

kawari hanazashi
(flower stitch variation)

Mark 3½in (9cm) square, with additional lines ¾in (2cm) in from the edges. Use a 2¾in (7cm) circle template to draw the pattern. Stitch wavy lines individually in rainbow order, starting with pink. Note: to tessellate this pattern, use a 2in (5cm) grid.

 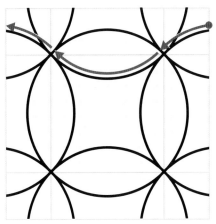

kawari hanazashi
(flower stitch variation)

Mark pattern 35. Stitch straight lines first in rainbow order, then stitch pattern 35 in white.

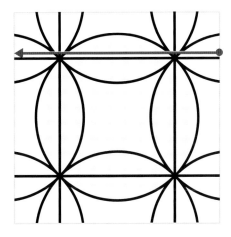 

Layered Circles

Variations on *shippō* (seven treasures) can include the foundation grid or extra diagonal lines. Focusing on different sections of the all-over *shippō* design makes either circular or flower-like designs.

37

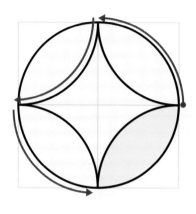

shippō
(seven treasures)

Mark 1½in (4cm) grid, 2 x 2 squares. Use a 3in (8cm) circle template to mark the pattern. Stitch around the pattern as shown, first in pink, then in peach.

38

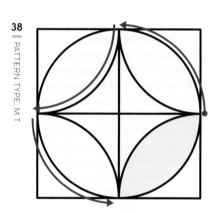

shippō
(seven treasures)

Mark pattern 37. Stitch the grid lines as pattern 25 in white, then stitch the overlapping curves as pattern 37, in pink.

39

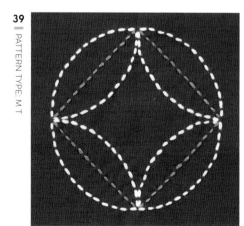

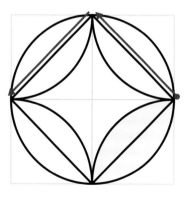

shippō
(seven treasures)

Mark pattern 37. Mark additional diagonal pattern lines as shown. Stitch the *shippō* motif, following pattern 37, then stitch the diagonal lines in pink.

Some of the oldest surviving Japanese textiles have shippō patterns. These are garments and Buddhist ritual textiles that were preserved in the Shōsō-in Imperial Repository in Nara after the death of Emperor Shōmu in 756CE, and they include the earliest known example of shippō stitched on shibori (tie dyed) silk.

shippō
(seven treasures)

Mark pattern 39. Stitch the grid lines as pattern 25 in white, then stitch the overlapping curves as pattern 37, in pink, and the diagonal lines in peach.

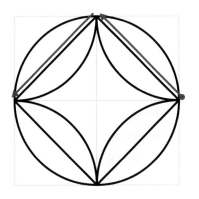
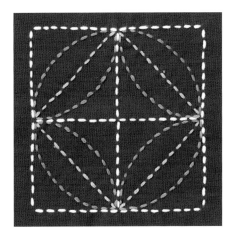

shippō
(seven treasures)

Mark 1½in (4cm) grid, 2 x 2 squares. Use a 3in (8cm) circle template to mark the pattern. Stitch as a series of intersecting arcs in rainbow order.

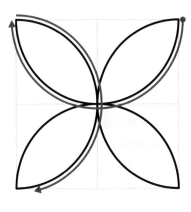

shippō
(seven treasures)

Mark pattern 41. Stitch the grid lines in white, then stitch the intersecting arcs as pattern 41, in pink.

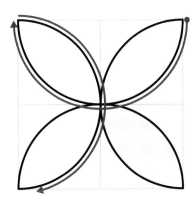

Layered Circles and Variations

Create bold variations on the *shippō* pattern by continuing to play with grids and diagonal lines, doubling up the curves to make woven effects, or adding small overlapping circles.

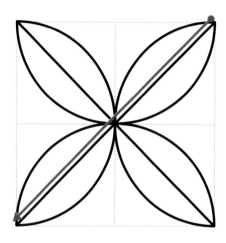

shippō
(seven treasures)

Mark pattern 41 and mark the additional diagonal pattern lines inside the overlapping curves as shown. Stitch the *shippō* motif as pattern 41, then stitch the diagonal lines, in pink and peach.

shippō
(seven treasures)

Mark pattern 43. Stitch the grid lines as pattern 25 in white, then stitch the arcs the same way as pattern 41, as shown in pink. Stitch the diagonal lines in peach and yellow.

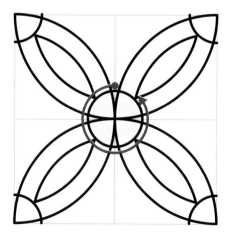

maru shippō
(circular seven treasures)

Mark pattern 48. Using a ¾in (2cm) circle template, draw a circle over the centre of the pattern, and arcs at the corners. Stitch the centre circle and corner arcs first, as shown in pink, then stitch the rest of the pattern in rainbow order but strand across the back of the centre circle, and don't stitch inside the corner arcs.

As in many cultures, the circle represents completeness, but also in Japanese Buddhism, goodness, perfection and enlightenment. An incomplete circle can represent wabi-sabi, the concept of imperfection. A circle is used instead of a tick when marking students' work, a cross for an incorrect answer, with the two marks known as 'maru batsu'.

maru shippō
(circular seven treasures)

Mark 1⅜in (3.5cm) grid, 2 x 2 squares. Use a 2¾in (7cm) circle template to draw the pattern lines and a ⅝in (1.5cm) circle template to mark the small circles as shown. Stitch the small circles first, as shown in pink, then stitch the rest of the pattern in rainbow order but strand across the back of the centre circle.

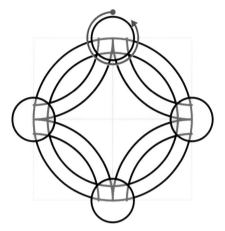 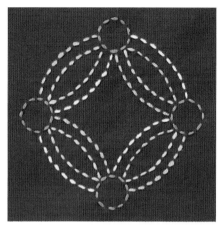

futate shippō
(double line seven treasures)

Mark pattern 37. Use a 2½in (6.5cm) circle template to mark a second line inside each curve, extending the lines at the edge of the pattern to make a woven effect around the edge, as shown. Stitch the pattern in rainbow order.

 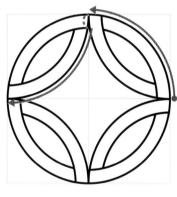

futate shippō
(double line seven treasures)

Mark pattern 41. Use a 2½in (6.5cm) circle template to mark a second line inside each curve, extending the lines at the edge of the pattern to make a woven effect around the edge, as shown. Stitch the pattern in rainbow order.

More Layered Circle Variations

Overlapping or superimposing more circles on top of the basic *shippō* design creates patterns that look complex but are actually quite simple to mark and stitch, while opening up many possibilities for pattern play.

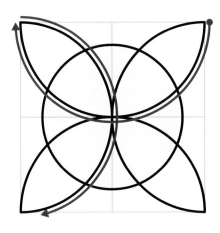

kawari shippō
(seven treasures variation)

Mark pattern 41. Mark an additional 2⅜in (6cm) circle centred on the pattern. Stitch the circle first, as shown in pink, then stitch pattern 41 in white.

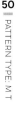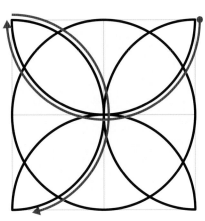

kawari shippō
(seven treasures variation)

Mark pattern 41. Mark an additional 3in (8cm) circle centred on the pattern. Stitch the circle first, as shown in pink, then stitch pattern 41 in white.

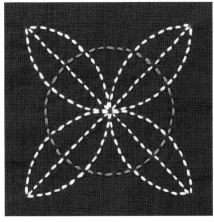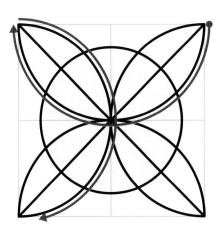

kawari shippō
(seven treasures variation)

Mark pattern 43. Mark an additional 2⅜in (6cm) circle centred on the pattern. Stitch the circle first, as shown in pink, then stitch pattern 43 in white.

kawari shippō
(seven treasures variation)

Mark pattern 43. Mark an additional 3in (8cm) circle centred on the pattern. Stitch the circle first, as shown in pink, then stitch pattern 43 in white.

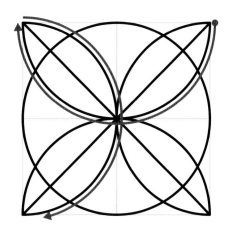

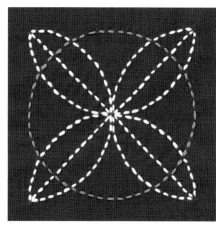

52
PATTERN TYPE: M T

kawari kasane shippō
(layered seven treasures variation)

Mark pattern 37. Mark pattern 41 over the top of this pattern. Stitch pattern 37, as shown in pink, then stitch pattern 41, as shown in white.

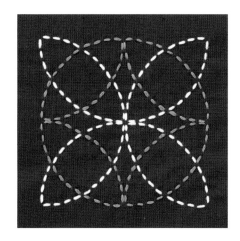

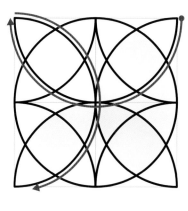

53
PATTERN TYPE: M T

There are many more variations on shippō than could be included here, made with additional lines or more overlapping circles, as can be seen here. It is a good pattern to return to and play around with in order to make up your total of 365 blocks, if you find some of the later designs too challenging! Here are a couple of extra ideas.

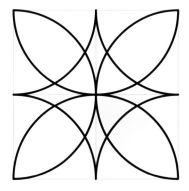

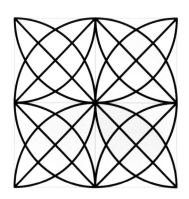

Linked Diamonds

The curved 'leaf' shapes in *shippō* designs can also be drafted as diamonds, becoming *hishi shippō* (diamond seven treasures) stitched in the same sequence.

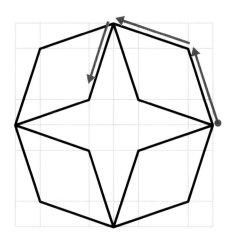

hishi shippō
(diamond seven treasures)

Mark ⅜in (1cm) grid, 8 x 8 squares. Note: the third and seventh vertical and horizontal grid lines do not need to be marked. Draw the diamond pattern. Stitch as a continuous line, as shown, in pink and peach.

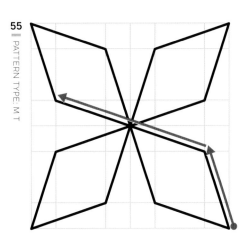

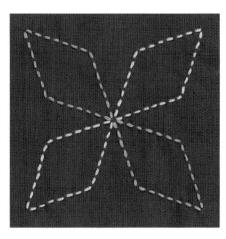

hishi shippō
(diamond seven treasures)

Mark grid as pattern 54. Draw the diamond pattern. Stitch as two diagonal diamond figures of eight, as shown, in pink and peach.

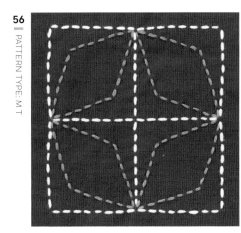

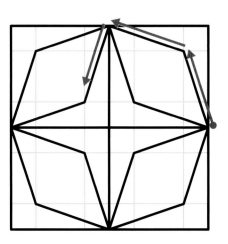

hishi shippō
(diamond seven treasures)

Mark grid as pattern 54. Mark diamond pattern as pattern 54. Stitch pattern 25 in white, then stitch the diamonds as pattern 54 in pink.

Hishi is not just a diamond or lozenge shape, but also the name for the water chestnut. But aren't water chestnuts round? Well, yes, but it refers to the shape of the leaf, which is like a diamond! As a design, the sideways stretched shape represents prosperity or increase.

hishi shippō
(diamond seven treasures)

Mark grid as pattern 54. Draw the diamonds as pattern 55. Stitch pattern 25 in white, then stitch the diamonds as pattern 55 in pink.

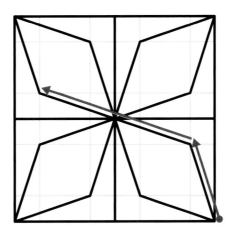

hishi shippō
(diamond seven treasures)

Mark pattern 54. Mark the diagonal lines linking the diamonds as a diagonal square. Stitch the diamonds as pattern 54 in white, then stitch the diagonal square in pink.

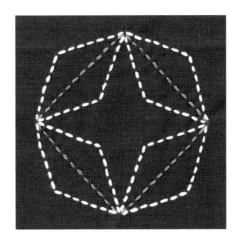
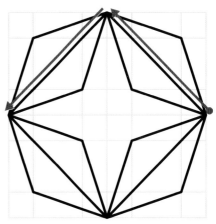

hishi shippō
(diamond seven treasures)

Mark pattern 55. Mark the diagonal lines linking the diamonds. Stitch the diamonds as pattern 55 in white, then stitch the diagonal lines in pink and peach.

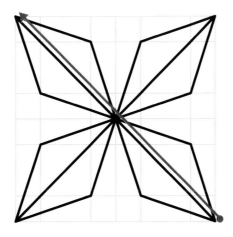
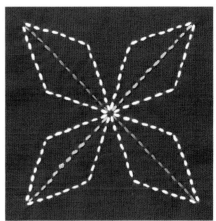

Sea Urchin

Ganzezashi is Tobishima (Tobi Island) dialect for 'sea urchin'. It is similar to *hishi shippō* patterns, but with multiple diagonal and gently curved lines that vary in number. Larger versions of the pattern can have even more lines.

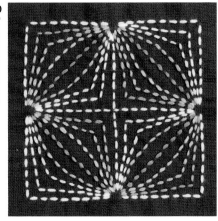

ganzezashi
(sea urchin stitch)

Mark pattern 56, plus diagonal lines from corner to corner, then use a 5in (12.5cm) circle template to mark the gently curved lines either side of the diagonal diamonds. Stitch pattern 25 in white, and the diagonal lines, as shown in pink. Leave a large gap where all the stitching lines meet. Stitch the remaining lines in rainbow order around the pattern.

ganzezashi
(sea urchin stitch)

Mark pattern 57, plus diagonal lines to make a square on point, then use a 5in (12.5cm) circle template to mark the gently curved lines as shown. Stitch pattern 25 in white, and the pattern lines on one diagonal as shown in rainbow order. Leave a large gap where all the stitching lines meet. Stitch the pattern lines on the remaining diagonal individually, as shown in white.

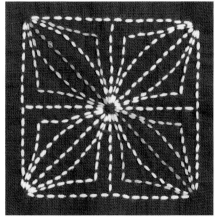

ganzezashi
(sea urchin stitch)

Mark ½in (1.3cm) grid, 6 x 6 squares, and mark additional lines at the ¼in (6mm) points as shown. Mark diagonals in each 1½in (4cm) square. Mark the diamonds, using the grid as a guide. Mark the arcs inside the diamonds using a 3½in (9cm) circle template. Stitch in a similar sequence to pattern 60, noting that there are fewer lines.

Tobishima (Tobi Island), the only inhabited island in the Sea of Japan, is near Sakata City. Although remote, it was on the Kitamaesen (North Sea route) during the Edo era (1603–1868CE), so exposed to the sophisticated kansai (Kyoto region) culture. Ganzezashi were often stitched on fishermen's donza (work coats) for protection.

dan ganzezashi
(stepped sea urchin stitch)

Mark ⅜in (1cm) grid, 8 x 8 squares. Mark a single diagonal line sloping up to the top left from bottom right, plus two short diagonal lines crossing this as shown. Mark the diamonds and arcs inside the diamonds, following pattern 62. Stitch the two squares, as shown in pink, filling in the lines in the squares in rainbow order. Then stitch the right angle lines, as shown in white.

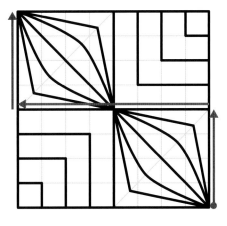
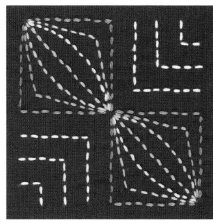

ganzezashi
(sea urchin stitch)

Mark grid as pattern 60, marking the gently curved lines only inside the diamonds. Stitch the diagonal lines in the diamonds in pink, then continue to stitch in rainbow order.

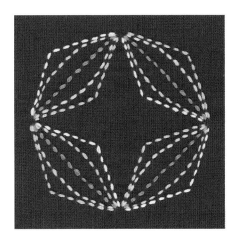
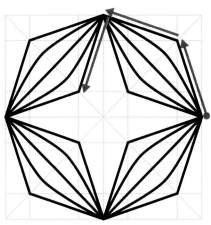

gazezashi
(sea urchin stitch)

Mark grid as pattern 61, marking the gently curved lines only inside the diamonds. Stitch the design as shown, in rainbow order.

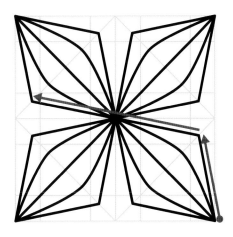
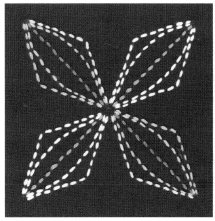

Diagonal Patterns

By centring on a different part of the design each time, these three diagonal patterns make six different blocks, with some looking like stars or flowers and others with a more circular effect.

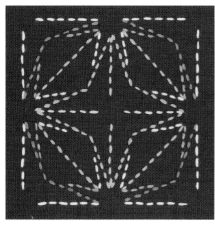

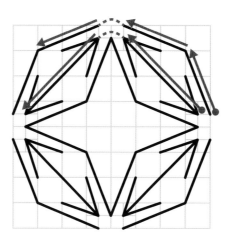

hana kaku shippō tsugnagi
(linked square seven treasures flower)

Mark ⅜in (1cm) grid, 8 x 8 squares, quartering the two squares on the centre of each side. Mark the diagonal lines as shown. Stitch the pattern lines in rainbow order, stranding across the back as shown.

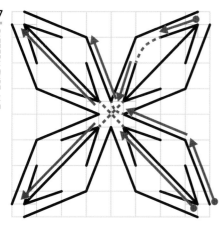

hana kaku shippō tsugnagi
(linked square seven treasures flower)

Mark ⅜in (1cm) grid, 8 x 8 squares, quartering the four squares in the centre and the square in each corner of the grid. Mark the diagonal lines as shown. Stitch the pattern lines in rainbow order, stranding across the back as shown.

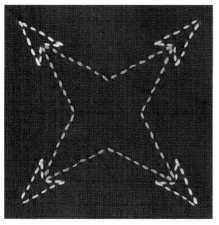

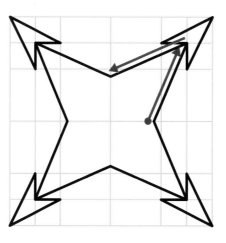

kaku hanazashi
(square flower stitch)

Mark ⅜in (1cm) grid, 8 x 8 squares. Note: the fourth and sixth vertical and horizontal grid lines do not need to be marked. Mark the pattern lines as shown. Stitch the central 'flower' first, then stitch the corner sections individually, in rainbow order.

These are all essentially variations on hishi shippō *(diamond seven treasures). While diamond and* shippō *patterns originally derive from aristocratic* yusoku *patterns of the Heian era (794–1185CE), many variations have been developed over the centuries and these are likely to be designs from the Edo era (1603–1868CE) .*

kaku hanazashi
(square flower stitch)

Mark ⅜in (1cm) grid, 8 x 8 squares. Note: the fourth and fifth vertical and horizontal grid lines do not need to be marked. Mark the pattern lines as shown. Stitch the centre as two figures of eight, in pink and peach, then stitch the corner sections individually, in rainbow order.

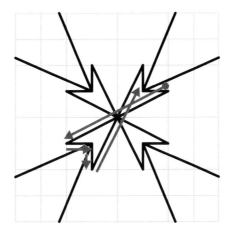 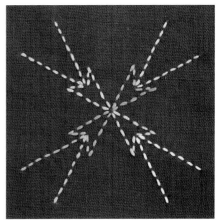

kawari kaku shippō
(square seven treasures variation)

Mark ⅜in (1cm) grid, 8 x 8 squares. Mark the pattern lines as shown. Stitch around the pattern, first in pink, and continuing in peach.

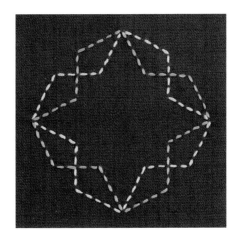 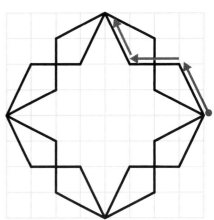

kawari kaku shippō
(square seven treasures variation)

Mark ⅜in (1cm) grid, 8 x 8 squares. Mark the pattern lines as shown. Stitch the first diagonal in pink, as a continuous figure of eight. Stitch the second diagonal in peach.

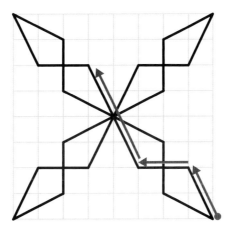 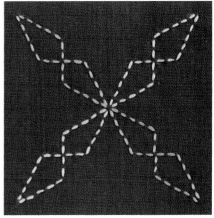

Crossed Wavy Lines

Marked with a grid and a circle, these designs are all very quick and easy to stitch, as is often the case for many patterns that take a little longer to draw! Pattern 74 has half the lines of pattern 33, *shippō tsunagi*.

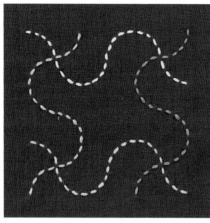
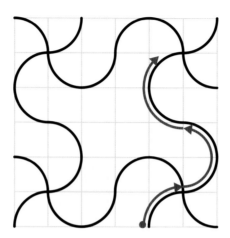

chidori
(plovers)

Mark ½in (1.3cm) grid, 6 x 6 squares. Mark the pattern lines as shown, using a 1in (2.5cm) circle template. Stitch each line individually, starting with pink and continuing in rainbow order.

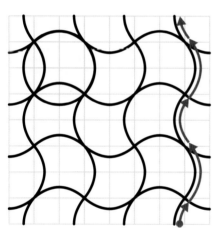
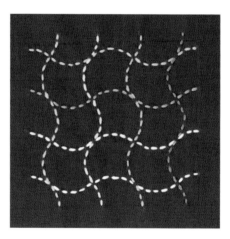

toridasuki
(crossed birds)

Mark ⅜in (1cm) grid, 8 x 8 squares. Mark the pattern lines as shown, using a 1in (2.5cm) circle template. Stitch each line individually, starting with the pink and continuing in rainbow order.

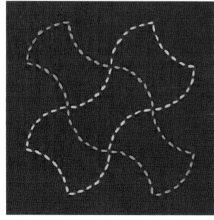
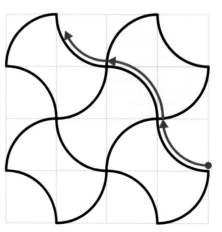

fundō
(scale weights)

Mark ¾in (2cm) grid, 4 x 4 squares. Mark the pattern lines as shown, using a 1½in (4cm) circle template. Stitch from corner to corner, starting with pink, then peach.

tokkuri ajiro
(sake bottle net)

Mark ¾in (2cm) grid 4 x 4 squares. Mark the pattern lines as shown, using a 1½in (4cm) circle template. Stitch from corner to corner, starting with the pink.

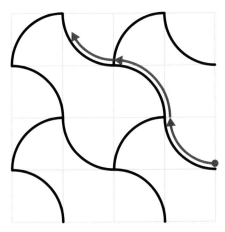
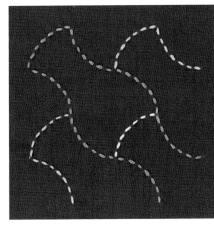

75 | PATTERN TYPE: M C

nagare manji
(flowing Buddhist manji)

Mark 1in x ¾in (2.5 x 2cm) grid, 4 x 4 rectangles. Mark the pattern lines as shown, using 2⅜in (6cm) and 2in (5cm) circle templates. Stitch each line individually, starting with pink and then continuing in rainbow order.

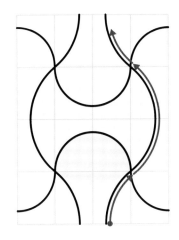

76 | PATTERN TYPE: M C

nagare manji
(flowing Buddhist manji)

Mark ½in x ⅜in (1.3cm x 1cm) grid, 8 x 8 rectangles. Mark the pattern lines as shown, using 1⅛in (3cm) and 1in (2.5cm) circle templates. Stitch each line individually, starting with pink and then continuing in rainbow order.

77 | PATTERN TYPE: M C

Clamshells and Waves

A basic clamshell becomes many different traditional patterns with extra lines added, including *nowaki* (grasses) and several *segaiha* (blue ocean wave) variations. Stitch from the bottom up to avoid turning loops on back.

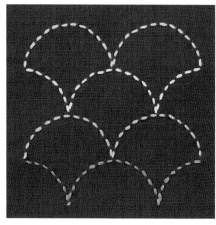

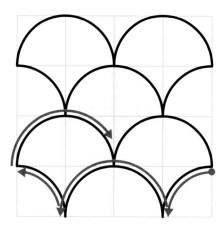

hamaguri no kai
(clamshell)

Mark ¾in (2cm) grid, 4 x 4 squares. Mark pattern lines as shown, using a 1½in (4cm) circle template. Stitch each line from the bottom edge upwards, starting with pink and continuing in rainbow order.

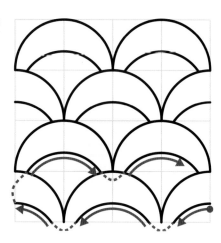

segaiha
(blue ocean wave)

Mark pattern 78, adding a second line arc approx. ¼in (6mm) above the horizontal grid line. Stitch the clamshells as pattern 78 in white. Stitch the additional lines of arcs in rainbow order, stranding across the back as shown.

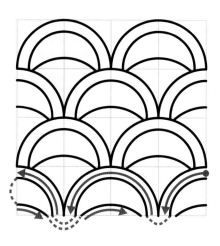

kawari segaiha
(blue ocean wave variation)

Mark pattern 78. Mark additional pattern lines as shown, using a 1⅛in (3cm) circle template. Stitch the clamshells as pattern 78 in white. Stitch additional lines in rainbow order, stranding across the back as shown.

Segaiha represents peace and good luck, named after a gagaku (ancient court music) dance of the Heian era (794–1185CE), where the costumes were decorated with it. Nowaki, which literally means 'icy autumn blast' but is usually translated as 'grasses', dates from the same era, and is said to have been inspired by a devastating typhoon.

kawari segaiha
(blue ocean wave variation)

Mark pattern 78. Mark additional pattern lines as shown, using 1⅛in (3cm) and ¾in (2cm) circle templates. Stitch the clamshells as pattern 78 in white. Stitch additional lines in rainbow order, stranding across the back as shown.

nowaki
(grasses)

Mark pattern 78. Pivot the circle template to draw the shorter grasses. Stitch the clamshells in rainbow order as shown, stranding across the back to change direction down to the base of the 'grass', before stitching over the top of the arc.

hamaguri no kai
(clamshell)

Mark pattern 78. Mark additional curves as shown, using a 2⅜in (6cm) circle template. Stitch the clamshells as pattern 78 in white. Stitch vertical lines in pink. Stitch remaining lines in rainbow order, stranding across the back as shown.

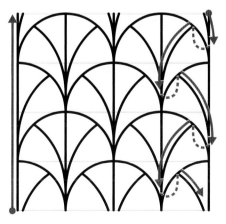

Waves and Nets

Use a circle template to draw these elegant wave and net patterns, which are easy to stitch. Their minimalistic style belies their ancient origins, especially *tatewaku* (rising steam), which is over a thousand years old.

PATTERN TYPE: M T

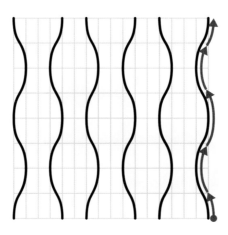

tatewaku
(rising steam)

Mark ⅜in x ³⁄₁₆in (1cm x 5mm) grid, 8 x 16 rectangles. Mark pattern lines as shown, using a 1½in (4cm) circle template. Stitch each line individually, starting with pink and continuing in rainbow order.

PATTERN TYPE: M T

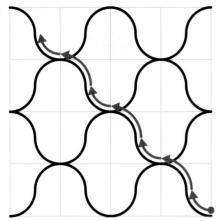

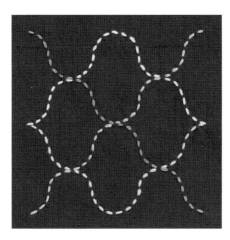

amimon
(net)

Mark ¾in (2cm) grid, 4 x 4 squares. Mark pattern lines as shown, using a ¾in (2cm) circle template. Stitch each line individually, starting with pink and then continuing in rainbow order.

PATTERN TYPE: M C

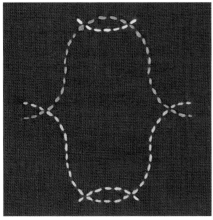

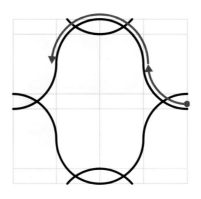

kasane amimon
(layered net)

Mark grid with ¾in (2cm) vertical lines and 1in (2.5cm) horizontal lines, then mark the additional ¼in (6mm) horizontal lines as shown. Mark pattern lines as shown, using a 1½in (4cm) circle template. Stitch each line individually, starting with pink and continuing in rainbow order.

Tatewaku dates from the Heian era (794–1185CE), and it symbolises rising above life's difficulties, like mist above a stream. Amimon originates from China, a symbol of luck for successful fishing, also representing gathering in wealth. Matsunami was also included in Hokusai's book, Shingata Komoncho (New Forms of Small Patterns).

kasane amimon
(layered net)

Mark grid as pattern 86. Mark pattern lines as shown, using a 1½in (4cm) circle template. Stitch each line individually, starting with pink and continuing in rainbow order.

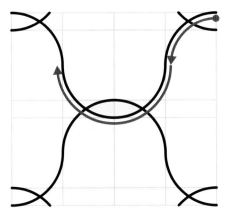
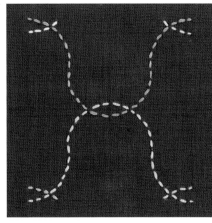

PATTERN TYPE: M C

matsunami
(pine wave)

Mark ⅜in (1cm) grid, 8 x 8 squares. Mark the arcs using a 1½in (4cm) circle template. Mark the small curves on the 'pine needles' freehand. Stitch arcs first, in pink and peach, then yellow, stranding at the back to stitch the small curves. Finish by stitching the blue and green lines, stranding across the back as before.

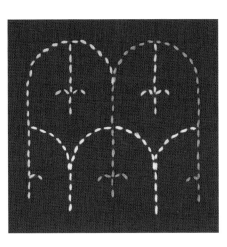
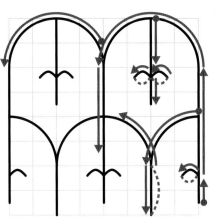

PATTERN TYPE: M T

segaiha
(blue ocean wave)

Mark 1½in (4cm) grid, 2 x 2 squares. Mark concentric arcs using 3in (8cm), 2½in (6.5cm), 2in (5cm), 1½in (3.5cm*) and 1in (2cm*) circle templates. *Note: circle sizes have been adjusted for simpler metric equivalents. Mark two or three short extra lines at the top of the pattern, to suggest pattern continuation (or omit if you prefer). Stitch in rainbow order.

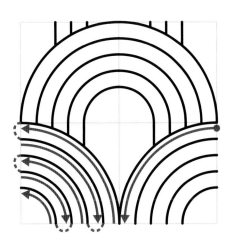
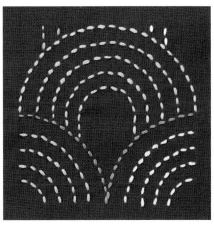

PATTERN TYPE: M T

Layered Arcs

Circle templates can be used to draw more complex arc designs, where the clamshell shape is turned in different directions, making a whole new set of patterns.

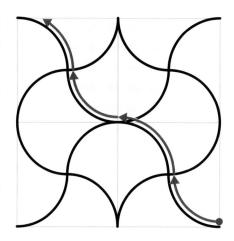

hamaguri tsunagi
(linked clam)

Mark ¾in (2cm) grid, 4 x 4 squares. Mark pattern lines as shown, using a 1½in (4cm) circle template. Stitch in rainbow order.

hanmaru tsunagi
(linked semicircles)

Mark pattern 90. Mark additional pattern lines as shown, using a ¾in (2cm) circle template to mark. Stitch pattern 90 in white, then stitch additional lines in rainbow order.

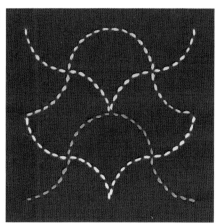
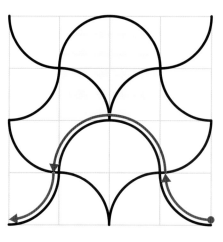

kawari hamaguri no kai
(clamshell variation)

Mark ¾in (2cm) grid, 4 x 4 squares. Mark pattern lines as shown, using a 1½in (4cm) circle template. Stitch in rainbow order.

Turning the arcs through 90 degrees brings new design possibilities. This kind of pattern was popular for kimono and obi in the 1960s and 1970s, and seems to reflect some of the contemporary 'mid-century modern' patterns popular at the time, both in the West and in Japan.

kawari segaiha
(blue ocean wave variation)

Mark pattern 92. Mark additional semicircles as shown, using a ¾in (2cm) circle template. Stitch pattern 92 in white, then stitch additional lines in pink and peach, stranding across the back as shown.

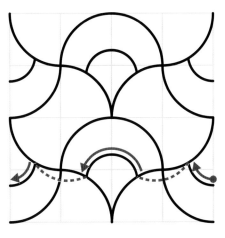
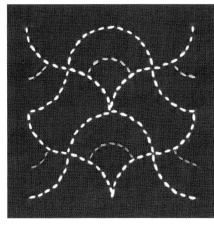

kawari segaiha
(blue ocean wave variation)

Mark pattern 90. Mark additional semicircles as shown, using a ¾in (2cm) circle template. Stitch pattern 90 in white, then stitch additional lines in rainbow order, stranding across the back as shown.

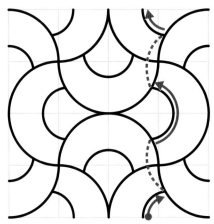

kawari segaiha
(blue ocean wave variation)

Mark pattern 94. Mark additional semicircles as shown, using a 1⅛in (3cm) circle template. Stitch pattern 94 in white, then stitch additional lines in rainbow order, stranding across the back as shown.

Sakata Patterns

These variations on the basic *shippō* (seven treasures) and *hishi shippō* (diamond seven treasures) patterns use different circle sizes or add extra lines to the basic motifs.

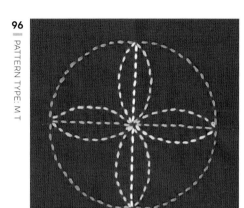

kawari shippō
(seven treasures variation)

Mark 1½in (4cm) grid, 2 x 2 squares. Mark pattern lines as shown, using a 3in (8cm) circle template for the outer circle and a 2in (5cm) circle template for the arcs. Stitch in rainbow order.

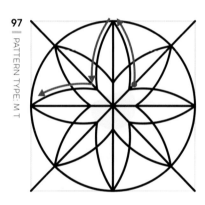

kawari shippō
(seven treasures variation)

Mark 1½in (4cm) grid, 2 x 2 squares. Mark pattern lines as shown, using a 3in (8cm) circle template for the outer circle and double arc star. Mark a circle using a ¾in (2cm) circle template in the centre, to align the ends of the arcs. Start by stitching the circle in pink and continue in rainbow order.

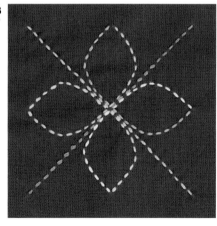

kawari shippō
(seven treasures variation)

Mark ¾in (2cm) grid, 4 x 4 squares. Mark pattern lines as shown, using a 3in (8cm) circle template to draw the 'petals' in two parts. Stitch the diagonal lines, first pink then peach, then continue in rainbow order, slightly rounding the tops of the 'petals'.

kawari shippō
(seven treasures variation)

Mark pattern 43. Mark additional pattern lines as shown, using a 3½in (9cm) circle template to draw the two overlapping ellipses. Stitch in rainbow order.

99

PATTERN TYPE: M T

kawari shippō
(seven treasures variation)

Mark 1in (2.5cm) grid, 3 x 3 squares, and mark a central line vertically and horizontally. Mark pattern lines as shown, using a 4½in (11.5cm) circle template to draw the two large overlapping ellipses and a 2⅜in (6cm) circle template to draw the small corner 'petals'. Stitch in rainbow order.

100

PATTERN TYPE: M T

kawari asanoha
(hemp leaf variation)

Mark pattern 59. Mark additional pattern lines as shown. Stitch the outline first in pink, then continue to stitch the diagonal lines in rainbow order.

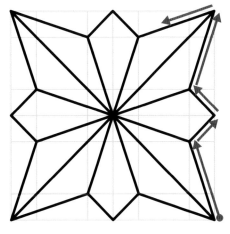
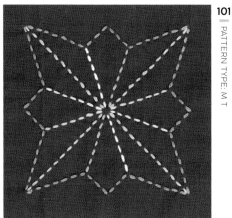

101

PATTERN TYPE: M T

Segmented Circles

A starry selection of designs including patterns inspired by pinwheels or windmills (*kazaguruma*). These could be tessellated within a grid of circles for an extended pattern.

hoshi
(star)

Mark 1½in (4cm) grid, 2 x 2 squares. Mark a 3in (8cm) circle as shown, using a 1in (2.5cm) circle at the centre. Draw lines through the centre at 30° angles, and link the outer points to the 1in (2.5cm) circle to make a star. Stitch the circle in pink and the star in peach.

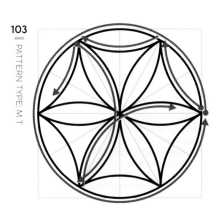

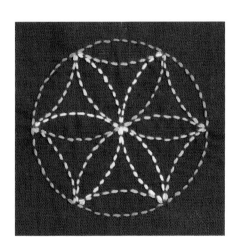

shippō kikkō
(hexagonal seven treasures)

Mark 1½in (4cm) grid, 2 x 2 squares. Mark a 3in (8cm) circle. Draw lines through the centre at 30° angles. Overlap a 3in (8cm) circle template to draw the pattern as shown. Stitch the circle in pink, the inner arcs in peach, and the remaining lines in rainbow order.

104

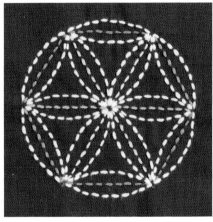

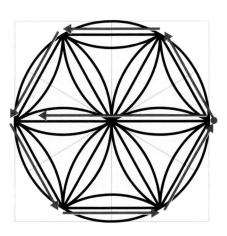

shippō kikkō
(hexagonal seven treasures)

Mark pattern 103. Mark additional pattern lines as shown. Stitch pattern 103 in white. Stitch the hexagon in pink, then continue to stitch the remaining lines in rainbow order.

Hoshi *and* shippō kikkō *designs are universal patterns, with the* shippō kikkō *stitched on antique* furoshiki *(wrapping cloths). The second* kazaguruma *design is from Shōnai, Yamagata, while the variations are my adaptations. Toy pinwheels are left spinning in the breeze at children's temple memorials.*

kazaguruma
(windmill)

Mark a 3in (8cm) square and a 3in (8cm) circle. Mark lines through the centre of the circle at 60° angles. Overlap a 2in (5cm) circle template on the lines to draw segments. Stitch the circle in pink, then continue to stitch in rainbow order.

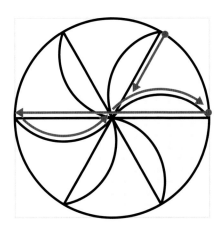 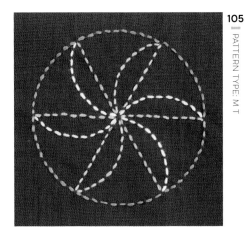

kazaguruma
(windmill)

Mark 1½in (4cm) grid, 2 x 2 squares. Mark a 3in (8cm) circle and mark diagonal lines through the centre as shown. Overlap a 2⅜in (6cm) circle template on the lines to draw segments. Stitch the circle in pink, then continue to stitch in rainbow order.

kazaguruma
(windmill)

Mark a 3in (8cm) square and a 3in (8cm) circle. Draw lines through the centre of the circle at 72° angles. Overlap a 2in (5cm) circle template to draw segments. Stitch the circle in pink, then continue to stitch in rainbow order.

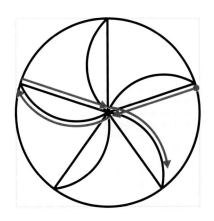 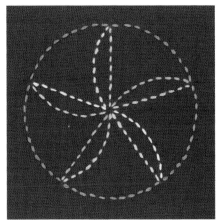

Layered Circle Motifs

Variations on the *shippō* (seven treasures) pattern, on a much smaller scale, add more designs to this family of patterns. The additional lines make them look like tiny leaves.

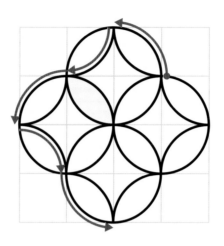

kawari shippō
(seven treasures variation)

Mark ¾in (2cm grid), 4 x 4 squares. Mark overlapping circles as shown, using a 1½in (4cm) circle template. Stitch around the design as shown in pink, then continue in rainbow order.

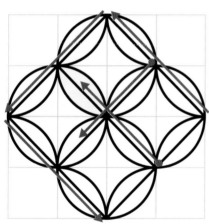

kawari shippō
(seven treasures variation)

Mark pattern 108. Mark additional diagonal lines as shown. Stitch pattern 108 in pink, then continue to stitch the diagonal lines in peach, yellow and green.

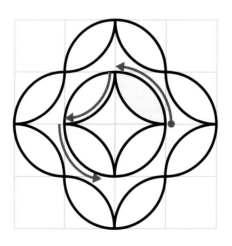

kawari shippō
(seven treasures variation)

Mark ¾in (2cm grid), 4 x 4 squares. Mark overlapping circles as shown, using a 1½in (4cm) circle template. Stitch around the outer section in pink and peach, then stitch the inner section in yellow and green.

There are seemingly endless possibilities with the basic circle overlap used for the shippō pattern. Turning the little 'leaf' shapes inwards creates a variety of stand-alone motifs, while using them as a kind of diagonal chain, as in patterns 112 and 113, can frame other elements in a sampler arrangement.

kawari shippō
(seven treasures variation)

Mark pattern 110. Mark additional diagonal lines as shown. Stitch pattern 110 in pink, then stitch the diagonal lines in peach and yellow.

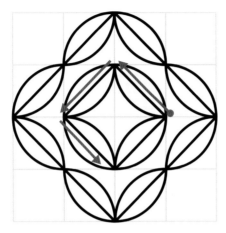

kawari shippō
(seven treasures variation)

Mark ¾in (2cm grid), 4 x 4 squares. Mark overlapping circles as shown, using a 1½in (4cm) circle template. Stitch the first pair of diagonal wavy lines in pink and peach as shown, then the second pair in yellow and green.

kawari shippō
(seven treasures variation)

Mark pattern 112. Mark additional diagonal lines as shown. Stitch the diagonal wavy lines in pink, and the straight diagonal lines in peach and yellow.

Leaf Patterns

The 'leaf' look of *shippō* (seven treasures) designs is even more pronounced when the patterns move away from circular arrangements and become more linear.

PATTERN TYPE: M T

kawari shippō
(seven treasures variation)

Mark ¾in (2cm grid), 4 x 4 squares. Mark leaf shapes as shown, using a 1½in (4cm) circle template. Stitch the diagonals in pink, then continue to stitch the pairs of 'leaves' around the edge in rainbow order.

PATTERN TYPE: M T

kawari shippō
(seven treasures variation)

Mark pattern 114. Mark additional diagonal lines as shown. Stitch pattern 114 in pink, then stitch the diagonal lines in rainbow order.

PATTERN TYPE: M T

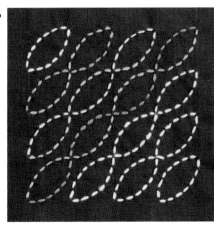

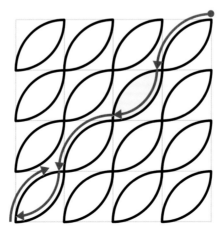

taikakusen kawari shippō
(diagonal seven treasures variation)

Mark ¾in (2cm grid), 4 x 4 squares. Mark leaf shapes as shown, using a 1½in (4cm) circle template. Stitch the long diagonal wavy lines first in pink and peach, then continue to stitch in rainbow order.

taikakusen kawari shippō
(diagonal seven treasures variation)

Mark pattern 116. Mark additional diagonal lines as shown. Stitch pattern 116 in pink, then continue to stitch the diagonal lines in rainbow order.

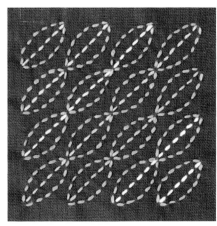

117

PATTERN TYPE: M T

noboru ha
(rising leaves)

Mark ¾in (2cm grid), 4 x 4 squares. Mark leaf shapes with a 1½in (4cm) circle template. For each row of leaves, stitch the vertical line first, as shown in pink, then the wavy lines, as shown in peach and yellow. Repeat to finish the pattern.

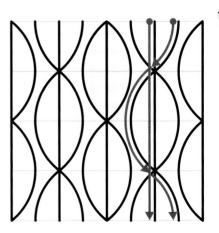

118

PATTERN TYPE: M T

kaku shippō
(square seven treasures)

Mark ¾in (2cm grid), 4 x 4 squares. Mark diagonal pattern lines as shown. Draw small *shippō* motifs, similar to pattern 96, using a 1⅛in (3cm) circle template. Stitch the overlapping diagonal rectangles in pink and peach first, then continue to stitch in rainbow order.

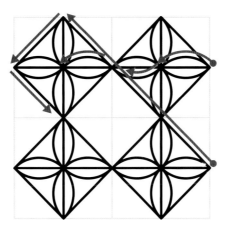
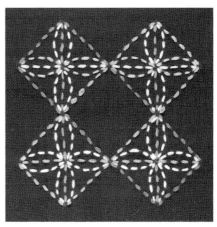

119

PATTERN TYPE: M T

Concentric Squares

Spirals and squares in squares patterns are among some of the very oldest sashiko designs, and all those featured here are stitched from the outside inwards.

 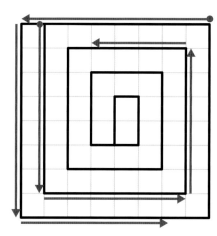

raimon or inazuma
(lightning spiral)

Mark ⅜in (1cm) grid, 8 x 8 squares. Stitch the outer square in pink, then stitch the spiral inwards from the top left in peach.

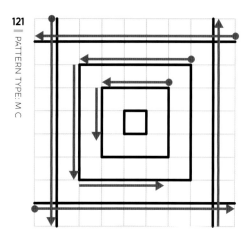 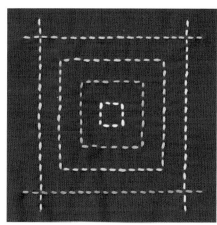

hiratsume san masu
(three concentric square measures)

Mark ⅜in (1cm) grid, 9 x 9 squares. Stitch the outer lines first, then each smaller square, in rainbow order.

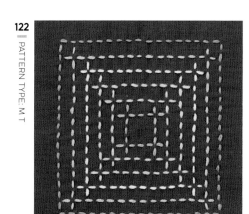 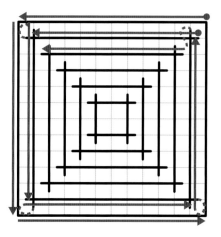

masuzashi
(square measure sashiko)

Mark ¼in (6mm) grid, 12 x 12 squares. Stitch the outer square in pink. Stitch each square spiralling towards the centre continuing in the rainbow order, crossing the corners by one stitch, and stranding across the back at the corners.

Popular choices for sashiko on noragi *(work jackets), traditionally the fabric was marked with a large grid and the pattern details skilfully placed by eye, without extra marking! When* masuzashi *or* hiratsume san masu *is stitched all over, a square on point pattern appears, in a similar way to Log Cabin patchwork designs.*

tsumeta
(boxed rice fields)

Mark ½in (1.3cm) grid, 6 x 6 squares. Mark the outer square ⅛in (3mm) in from the outer grid line. Stitch in rainbow order.

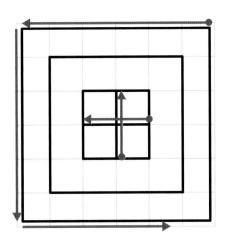

hiratsume san masu
(three concentric square measures)

Mark ⅜in (1cm) grid, 8 x 8 squares. Stitch the outer square in pink, then stitch in rainbow order.

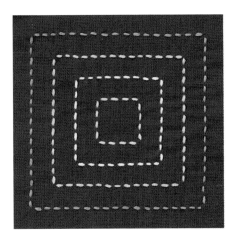

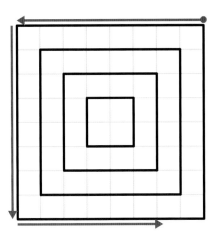

taikakusen kawari shippō
(diagonal seven treasures variation)

Mark pattern 124. Mark additional diagonal lines as shown. Stitch the diagonal lines in pink and peach, then stitch pattern 124 in white.

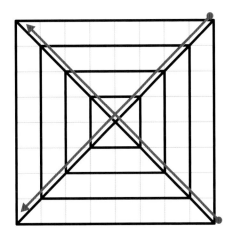

Screen Grids

The simplest grid patterns of *kumiko* (latticework) on papered *shōji* screens make an interesting alternative to a simple square grid, and these have many named variations.

126

PATTERN TYPE: M T

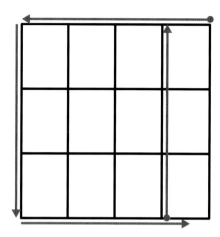

aragumi shōji
(simple screen)

Mark 1in x ¾in (2.5cm x 2cm) grid, 3 x 4 rectangles. Stitch the outer square in white, then stitch the lines in rainbow order.

127

PATTERN TYPE: M T

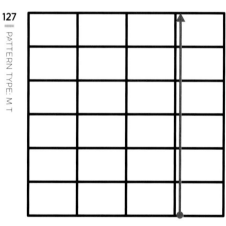

yokogumi shōji
(horizontal stile screen)

Mark ½in x ¾in (1.3cm x 2cm) grid, 6 x 4 rectangles. Stitch the outer square in white, then stitch the lines in rainbow order.

128

PATTERN TYPE: M T

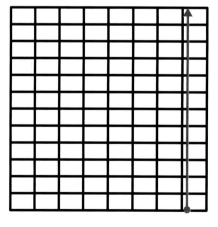

honshige shōji
(very narrow screen)

Mark ¼in x ⅜in (6mm x 1cm) grid, 12 x 8 rectangles. Stitch the outer square in white, then stitch the lines in rainbow order. Note: there is only space for one stitch in each vertical line section and two in each horizontal line section.

Lightweight wooden shōji screens, papered with tough washi mulberry fibre paper, are a ubiquitous element of Japanese interior décor, sliding for ventilation or to open up one room to another, running in shallow tracks. Their traditional size is similar to a tatami mat, giving a subtle rhythm to interiors.

yokoshige shōji
(horizontal narrow screen)

Mark ¼in x ¾in (6mm x 2cm) grid, 12 x 4 rectangles. Stitch the outer square in white, then stitch the lines in rainbow order. Note: there is only space for one stitch in each vertical line section.

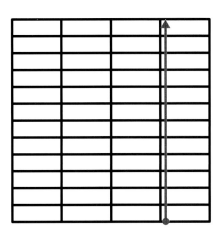
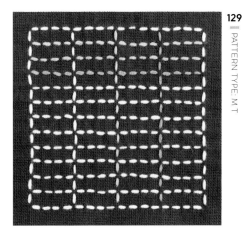

129

PATTERN TYPE: M T

tateshige shōji
(vertical narrow screen)

Mark 1in x ¼in (2.5cm x 6mm) grid, 3 x 12 rectangles. Stitch the outer square in white, then stitch the lines in rainbow order. Note: there is only space for one stitch in each horizontal line section.

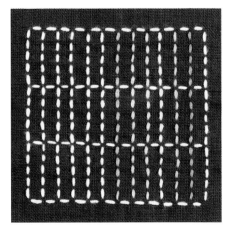
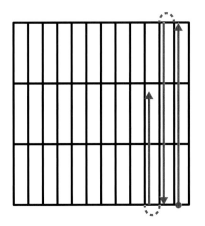

130

PATTERN TYPE: M T

fukiyose shōji
(gathered screen)

Mark 1in x ½in grid (2.5cm x 1.3cm), 3 x 6 rectangles. Mark additional vertical lines ¹⁄₁₆in (1.5mm) at either side of the second, fourth and sixth vertical grid lines. Stitch the outer square in white, then stitch the vertical lines first in rainbow order, then stitch the horizontal lines. Note: in horizontal sections, space for stitches alternates between two stitches and one stitch.

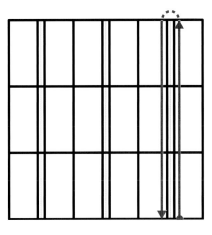
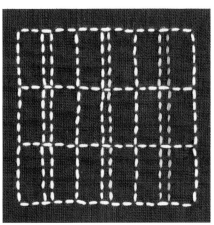

131

PATTERN TYPE: M T

Woven Squares

Extra lines added to basic grids create a range of woven effects, which look just as effective over a small square as when filling a larger area.

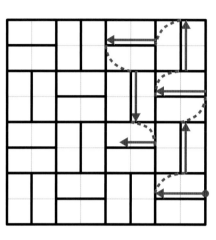

nikuzushi mon
(two break pattern)

Mark ⅜in (1cm) grid, 8 x 8 squares. Stitch pattern 19 in white, then stitch the remaining lines in rainbow order, stranding across the back between the horizontal and vertical lines, as shown.

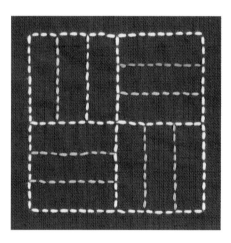

hirasan kuzushi
(simple three lines form)

Mark ½in (1.3cm) grid, 6 x 6 squares. Stitch pattern 25 in white, then stitch the remaining lines in rainbow order, stranding across the back between lines.

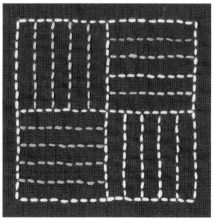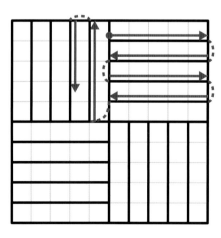

taikakusen kawari shippō
(diagonal seven treasures variation)

Mark 1½in (4cm) grid, 4 x 4 squares. Use a ruler to mark additional lines ⅓in (8mm) apart, dividing each square into five long strips. Stitch pattern 25 in white, then stitch the remaining lines in rainbow order, stranding across the back between lines.

Smaller shōji screens, covering internal wall openings or windows, often have more elaborate patterns than their door-sized cousins. They may echo other architectural elements like the irori *(sunken hearth) in a four-and-a-half tatami mat room, where the hearth is in the centre of the four mats.*

tsumiki
(building blocks)

Mark ½in (1.3cm) grid, 6 x 6 squares. Mark diagonal pattern lines as shown. Stitch pattern 25 in white, as well as the diagonal lines. Stitch the remaining lines in rainbow order, stranding across the back between lines, as shown.

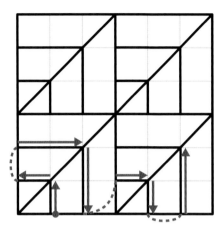
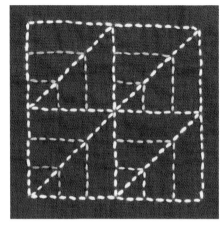

irori
(sunken hearth)

Mark ½in (1.3cm) grid, 6 x 6 squares. Stitch pattern 25 in white, then stitch the remaining lines in rainbow order, stranding across the back between lines.

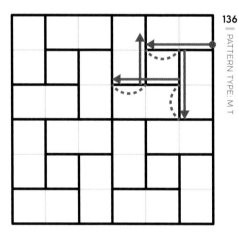

kakuyose
(intersecting square corners)

Mark ⅜in (1cm) grid, 7 x 7 squares with a half square at each edge. Stitch the whole squares first, in pink and peach, then stitch the remaining lines in rainbow order.

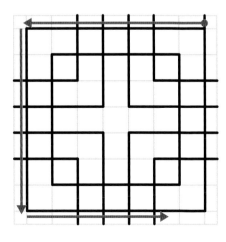
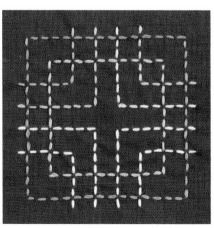

Woven Effects

The optical effect of an open weave is created with multiple lines enclosing empty squares, while focusing on different parts of the pattern makes more than one block.

138

PATTERN TYPE: M T

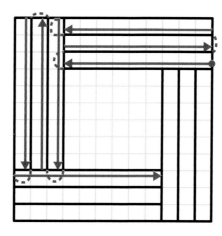

igeta koshi
(well curb check)

Mark ¼in (6mm) grid, 12 x 12 squares (only the four outer lines are really necessary all round, but marking the whole grid is easier). Stitch around the outer square first, in pink, then continue to stitch the remaining lines in rainbow order, filling in each section.

139

PATTERN TYPE: M T

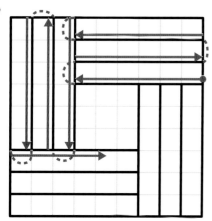

kawari igeta koshi
(well curb check variation)

Mark ⅜in (1cm) grid, 9 x 9 squares. Stitch around the outer square first, in pink, then continue to stitch the remaining lines in rainbow order, filling in each section.

140

PATTERN TYPE: M T

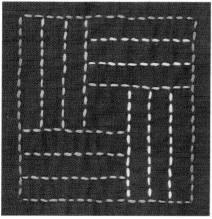

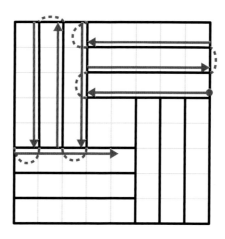

ishidatami
(paving block)

Mark ⅜in (1cm) grid, 8 x 8 squares. Stitch as pattern 139.

A striking detail in traditional Japanese architecture is the ceiling, which is often panelled or covered in a woven bamboo or thin wood in designs such as these. Also seen in basketry and straw matting, these patterns are copied to decorate ceramics, fabric and paper – a rich resource indeed.

ishidatami
(paving block)

Mark ⅜in (1cm) grid, 9 x 9 squares. Stitch each long section in rainbow order (pink, peach, yellow), stranding across the back between lines, as shown, then stitch the shorter lines in the same way, continuing with the rainbow order.

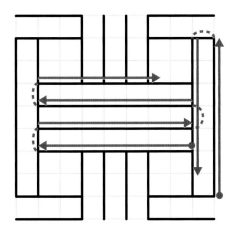 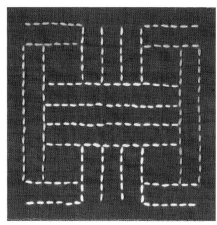

141

PATTERN TYPE: M C

ajiro
(wickerwork)

Mark ⅜in (1cm) grid, 8 x 8 squares. Stitch each long section in rainbow order (pink, peach, yellow, green), stranding across the back between lines, then stitch the shorter lines in the same way, continuing with the rainbow order.

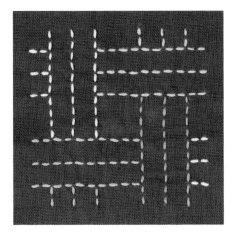 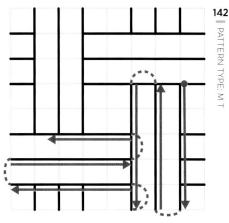

142

PATTERN TYPE: M T

ajiro
(wickerwork)

Mark ⅜in (1cm) grid, 8 x 8 squares. Stitch each long section in rainbow order (pink, peach, yellow), stranding across the back between lines, then stitch the shorter lines in the same way, continuing in rainbow order.

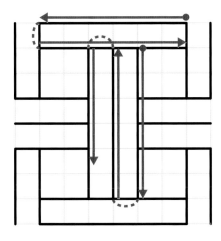 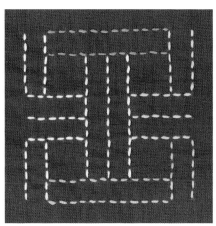

143

PATTERN TYPE: M T

Well Curbs

The well curb, a cross that looks very much like a hashtag (#) sign, is a popular motif for *kasuri* (double ikat) fabric, and *shokkō nishiki*, a Chinese brocade design.

PATTERN TYPE: M C

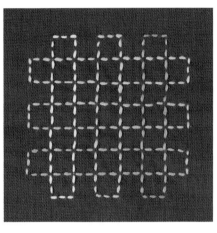

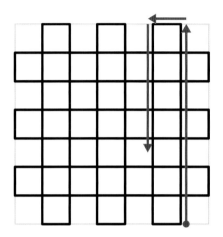

koshi kasuri
(ikat check)

Mark ⅜in (1cm) grid, 7 x 7 squares. Stitch each section individually, in rainbow order. Note: when this pattern is tessellated, it alternates with a plain square in a checkerboard.

145

PATTERN TYPE: M T

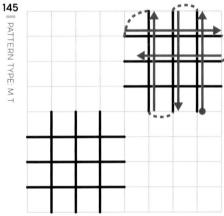

hirai jūmon
(crossed well curb)

Mark ⅜in (1cm) grid, 8 x 8 squares. Stitch each small grid motif in rainbow order, stranding across the back at the end of each line.

146

PATTERN TYPE: M T

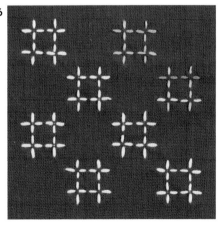

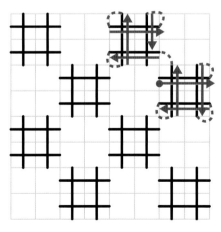

igeta
(well curb)

Mark ⅜in (1cm) grid, 8 x 8 squares. Mark *igeta* (well curb) motifs using the grid as a guide, with lines ⅜in (5mm) apart. Stitch each *igeta* motif individually, in rainbow order, stranding across the back at the corners.

Kasuri *(double ikat) fabric was imported after Japan's invasion of the Ryukyu Kingdom (now Okinawa) in 1609, where it had been a traditional technique since the 12th century. Warp or weft threads, or both for* igeta *patterns, are resist dyed before weaving. It is labour intensive and expensive, and simultaneously chic yet rustic.*

yae tsuno shokkō
(horned shokkō brocade)

Mark ½in (1.3cm) grid, 7 x 7 squares. Mark diagonal lines as shown. Stitch *igeta* (well curb) motifs individually, as for pattern 146, in white. Stitch diagonal lines in rainbow order, stranding behind the *igeta* motifs.

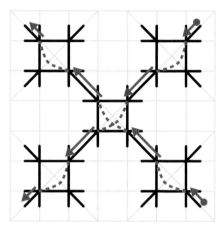
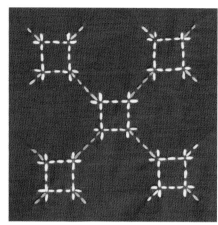

yae tsuno shokkō
(horned shokkō brocade)

Mark ½in (1.3cm) grid, 7 x 7 squares. Mark diagonal lines as shown. Stitch *igeta* (well curb) motifs individually, as for pattern 146, in white. Stitch diagonal lines in rainbow order, stranding behind the *igeta* motifs.

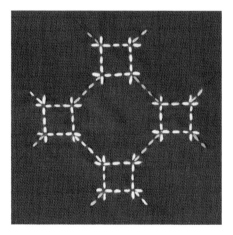
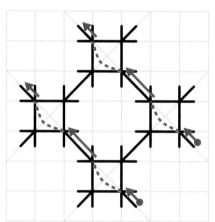

kawari yae tsuno shokkō
(horned shokkō brocade variation)

Mark 1½in (4cm) grid, 2 x 2 squares. Mark diagonal lines as shown and *igeta* (well curb) motifs, with lines ¼in (6mm) from the edge of the grid. Stitch *igeta* motifs in pink. Stitch diagonal lines continuing in rainbow order, stranding behind the *igeta* motifs.

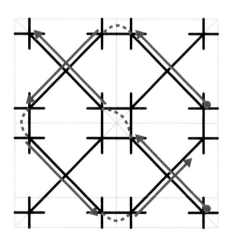
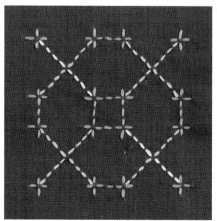

Complex Screens

These designs are used for fancy versions of *kumiko* (latticework) on screens such as *ranma* (the transom above *shōji* sliding screens). Each one begins as pattern 25.

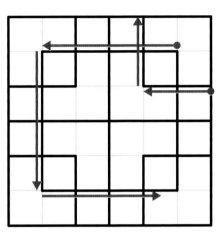

kaku tsunagi
(linked angles)

Mark ½in (1.3cm) grid, 6 x 6 squares. Stitch pattern 25 in white. Stitch the inner square in pink, then stitch the corner angles individually, in rainbow order.

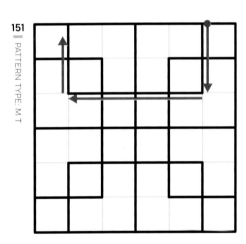

kaku tsunagi
(linked angles)

Mark ½in (1.3cm) grid, 6 x 6 squares. Stitch pattern 25 in white, then stitch each section individually, in rainbow order.

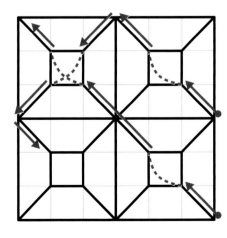

yotsuba kaku tsunagi
(quatrefoil linked angles)

Mark ½in (1.3cm) grid, 6 x 6 squares. Mark diagonal pattern lines as shown. Stitch pattern 25 in white. Stitch squares individually in pink, then stitch diagonal lines in rainbow order, stranding across the back of the squares.

yotsuba igeta tsunagi
(quatrefoil linked well curbs)

Mark ½in (1.3cm) grid, 6 x 6 squares. Mark diagonal pattern lines as shown. Stitch pattern 25 in white. Stitch *igeta* (well curb) motifs individually in pink as pattern 146. Stitch diagonal lines in rainbow order, stranding behind the *igeta* motifs.

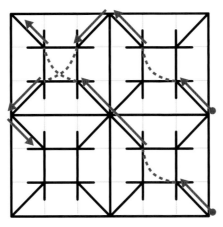 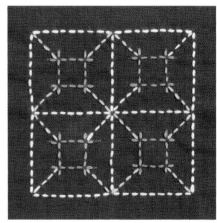

shokkō kaku tsunagi
(linked squares shokkō brocade)

Mark ½in (1.3cm) grid, 6 x 6 squares. Mark diagonal pattern lines as shown. Stitch the pink line first, then peach, crossing the lines at the centre, then stitch the remaining lines in rainbow order.

 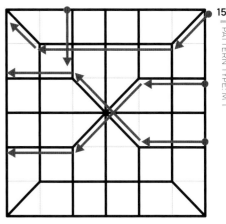

shokkō kaku tsunagi
(linked squares shokkō brocade)

Mark ½in (1.3cm) grid, 6 x 6 squares. Mark diagonal pattern lines as shown. Stitch pink lines first, then peach, then stitch the remaining lines in rainbow order.

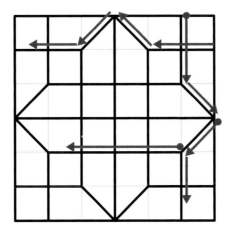 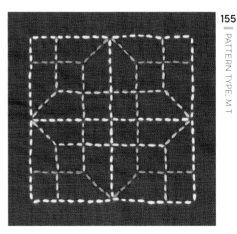

Well Curbs and Checks

Igeta or *izutsu* (well curb) motifs are closely related to *tsuno* (horned) patterns, where the corners also cross. *Koshi tsunagi* (linked check) and *renji kumiko* (vertical latticework) are also easy grid-based patterns.

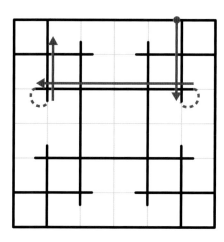

izutsu tsunagi
(linked well curb)

Mark ½in (1.3cm) grid, 6 x 6 squares. Stitch the outer square in white. Stitch each inner section individually, in rainbow order, crossing the corners.

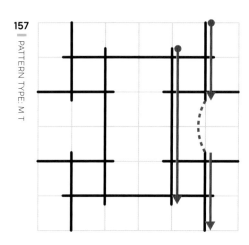

izutsu kiriko tsunagi
(cut linked well curb)

Mark ½in (1.3cm) grid, 6 x 6 squares. Stitch lines individually, in rainbow order, stranding across the back where shown.

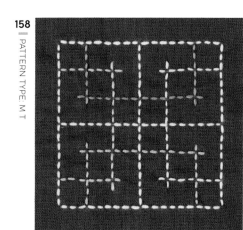
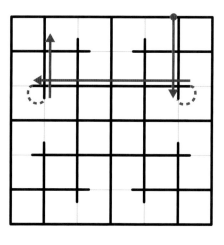

tsuno kaku tsunagi
(horned linked angles)

Mark ½in (1.3cm) grid, 6 x 6 squares. Stitch pattern 25 in white. Stitch each section individually, in rainbow order, crossing the corners as shown.

As seen in the two versions of koshi tsunagi included, focusing on different areas of a larger pattern can create two different sashiko samples; while the additional grid lines are the main difference between patterns 156 (izutsu tsunagi) and 158 (tsuno kaku tsunagi), and pattern 157 (izutsu kiriko tsunagi).

koshi tsunagi
(linked check)

Mark ½in (1.3cm) grid, 6 x 6 squares. Mark diagonal pattern line as shown. Stitch the square and the diagonal line in pink, then stitch the remaining lines in rainbow order.

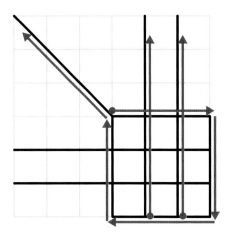

159 PATTERN TYPE: M T

koshi tsunagi
(linked check)

Mark ½in (1.3cm) grid, 7 x 7 squares. Mark diagonal pattern line as shown. Stitch the vertical and horizontal lines in rainbow order (pink, peach, yellow, green), then stitch the diagonal line and half way around the square in blue and the other half of the square in lilac as shown.

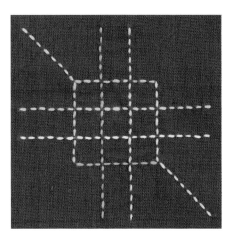
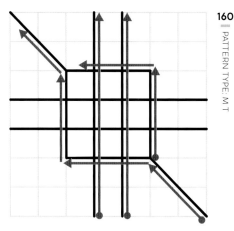

160 PATTERN TYPE: M T

renji kumiko
(vertical latticework)

Mark ⅜in (1cm) grid, 8 x 8 squares. Stitch the outer square in pink. Stitch the vertical lines (peach, yellow, green), then the horizontal lines (blue, lilac). Stitch remaining square zigzag in white.

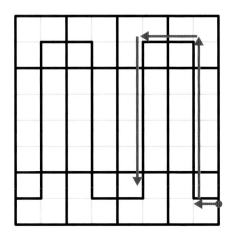
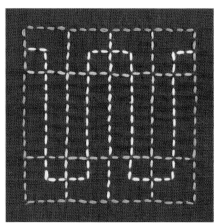

161 PATTERN TYPE: M T

Screen Patterns

Sopisticated objects such as *soroban* (abacus), *shokkō* (shokkō brocade), *mage kōzō* (bent 'incense' symbol pattern) and *matsuba* (pine needles) have all inspired *shōji* screen grids.

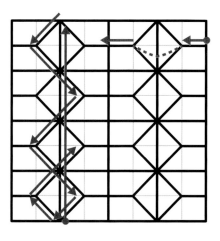

soroban dama
(abacus beads)

Mark ⅜in (1cm) grid, 8 x 8 squares. Mark the diagonal pattern lines for the 'beads'. Stitch pattern 25 in white. Stitch vertical lines in pink, then stitch diagonal lines and horizontal lines in rainbow order.

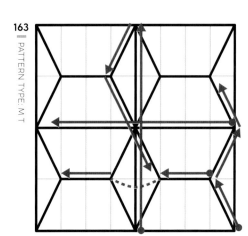

soroban kuzushi
(modified abacus)

Mark ¾in x ⅜in (2cm x 1cm) grid, 4 x 8 rectangles. Stitch around outer square in white. Stitch zigzags in pink. Stitch central vertical line in peach, then continue in rainbow order, stranding across the back where shown.

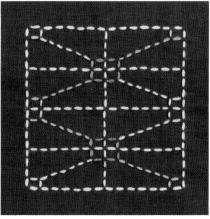

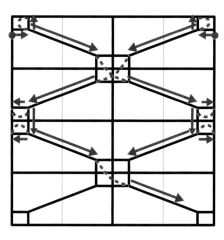

shokkō
(shokkō brocade)

Mark ¾in x 1½in (2cm x 4cm) grid, 4 x 2 rectangles. Mark 'boxes' at corners of rectangles ³⁄₁₆in x ¼in (5mm x 6mm). Link box corners with diagonals. Stitch white lines. Stitch central boxes individually in pink. Stitch side boxes and diagonals in peach and yellow.

tsuno shokkō
(horned shokkō brocade)

Mark pattern 164. Extend box lines to make *igeta* (well curb) motifs. Stitch white lines as shown. Stitch central *igeta* individually in pink. Stitch side *igeta* and diagonals in peach and yellow.

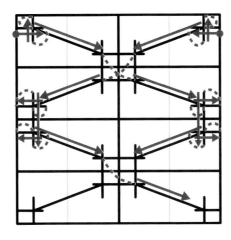

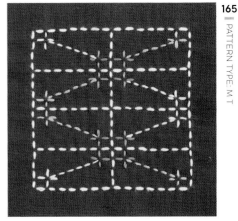

165

PATTERN TYPE: M T

mage kōzō
(bent 'incense' symbol pattern)

Mark ⅜in (1cm) grid, 8 x 8 squares. Mark the pattern lines, slightly curving some as shown. Stitch the outer square in white, then stitch the inner lines in rainbow order.

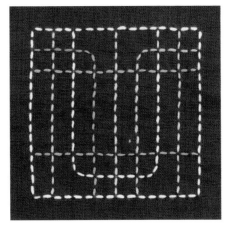

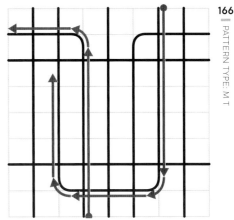

166

PATTERN TYPE: M T

matsuba tsunagi
(linked pine needles)

Mark a 3in (8cm) square, with vertical lines ⅜in (1cm) apart. Mark a central horizontal line, with two lines ⅛in (3mm) above and below it. Mark ¼in (6mm) horizontal lines at the top and bottom of the square. Mark diagonal pattern lines as shown. Stitch continuous zigzags in pink and peach, then continue to stitch the horizontal lines in rainbow order.

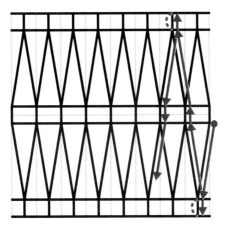

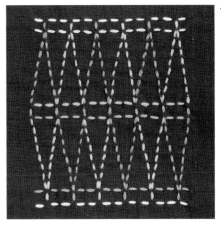

167

PATTERN TYPE: M T

Persimmon and Coins

The larger versions of these patterns have stepped lines. Later, they are included as *hitomezashi* (one stitch sashiko), where straight verticals and horizontals meet to make the pattern.

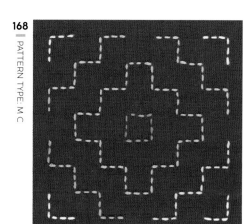
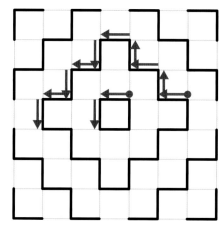

kakinohanazashi
(persimmon flower stitch)

Mark ½in (1.3cm) grid, 7 x 7 squares. Stitch centre square in pink, then stitch outwards in rainbow order.

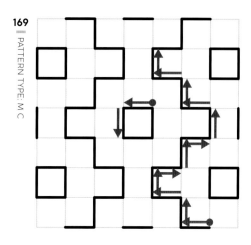

kakinohanazashi tsunagi
(linked persimmon flower stitch)

Mark ½in (1.3cm) grid, 7 x 7 squares. Stitch centre square in pink, then stitch horizontal stepped lines in peach and yellow, and continue in rainbow order.

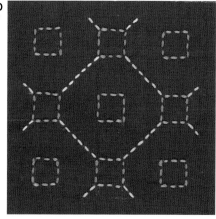
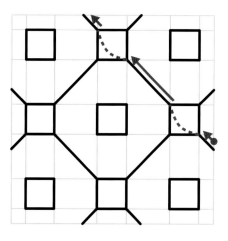

zenizashi
(coin stitch)

Mark ½in (1.3cm) grid, 7 x 7 squares. Mark diagonal pattern lines as shown. Stitch squares individually in pink, then stitch diagonal lines in rainbow order.

In Japan, the persimmon tree and its fruits are as ubiquitous as the apple in the West. Associated with good luck, longevity and perfection, its flower has four petals and the fruits are round but squarish. Zenizashi was stitched as a wish for wealth, resembling coins with holes in the centre.

kawari zenizashi
(coin stitch variation)

Mark ½in (1.3cm) grid, 5 x 5 squares, plus additional line ¼in (6mm) all round. Mark diagonal pattern lines as shown. Stitch squares and partial squares individually in pink, then diagonal lines in rainbow order.

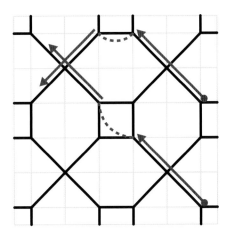 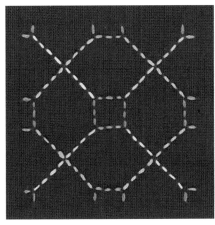

jōkaku
(castellation)

Mark ½in (1.3cm) grid, 7 x 7 squares. Stitch stepped lines in rainbow order.

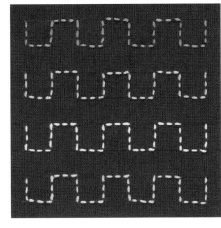 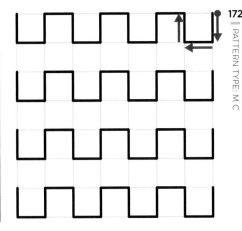

jūji
(crosses)

Mark ½in (1.3cm) grid, 7 x 7 squares. Stitch individual crosses in rainbow order.

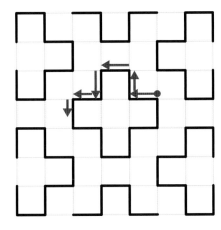 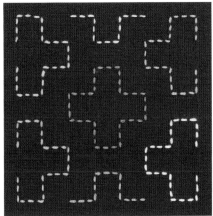

Steps and Arrows

Stepped lines can be given different spacing and arrangements to make a variety of designs. With the addition of diagonal lines, steps become arrow feathers.

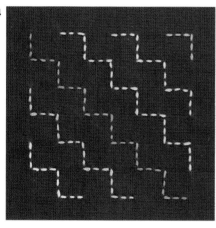

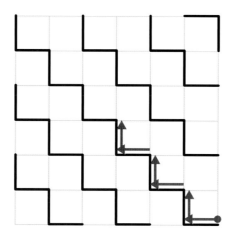

dan tsunagi
(linked steps)

Mark ½in (1.3cm) grid, 6 x 6 squares. Stitch each stepped line individually, starting with the longest line in pink and continuing in rainbow order.

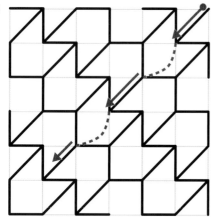

yabane
(arrow feather)

Mark ½in (1.3cm) grid, 6 x 6 squares. Mark diagonal pattern lines as shown. Stitch pattern 174 in white. Stitch diagonal lines individually in rainbow order, stranding across the back as shown.

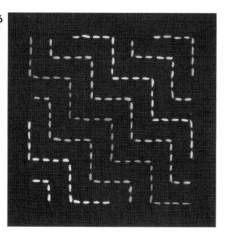

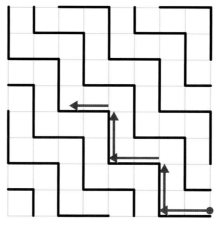

dan tsunagi
(linked steps)

Mark ⅜in (1cm) grid, 8 x 8 squares. Stitch each stepped line individually, starting with the longest line in pink and continuing in rainbow order.

dan tsunagi
(linked steps)

Mark pattern 176. Mark an additional set of stepped lines in between, ³⁄₁₆in (5mm) apart. Stitch each stepped line individually, starting with the longest line in pink and continuing in rainbow order.

177
PATTERN TYPE: M C

kawari dan tsunagi
(linked steps variation)

Mark ½in (1.3cm) grid, 8 x 8 squares. Mark an additional set of stepped lines ³⁄₁₆in (5mm) apart. Stitch central cross in pink and peach, and continue to stitch stepped lines in rainbow order.

178
PATTERN TYPE: M C

kawari dan tsunagi
(linked steps variation)

Mark ½in (1.3cm) grid, 7 x 7 squares. Mark an additional set of stepped lines ³⁄₁₆in (5mm) apart. Stitch pink and peach stepped lines first, then continue with the rainbow order (each section has been shown in a different thread colour, rather than individual pattern lines).

179
PATTERN TYPE: M C

Small Steps

Stepped patterns work on a smaller scale as *hitomezashi* (one stitch sashiko) patterns, starting with the same variation on *yokogushi* (horizontal rows) (see Techniques: Warm Up Stitching Exercise).

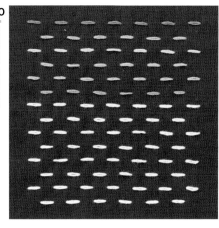

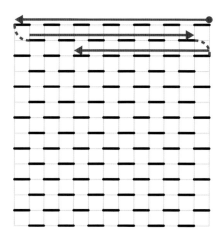

yokogushi
(horizontal rows)

Mark ¼in (6mm) grid, 13 x 13 squares. Stitch horizontal rows in rainbow order, alternating the stitches and gaps between each row. Strand across the back from one row to the next.

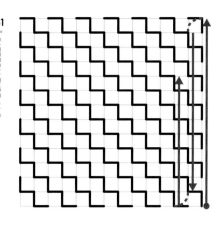

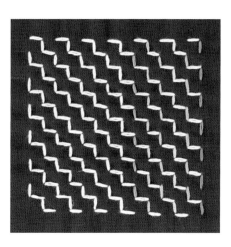

kaidan tsunagi
(linked staircase)

Mark and stitch pattern 180 in white. Stitch vertical rows in rainbow order, meeting the ends of the previous stitches but keeping the lines straight, and alternating the stitches and gaps between each row.

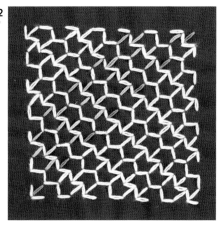

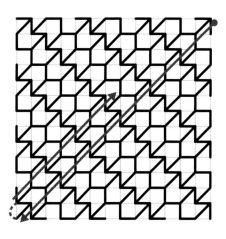

yabane
(arrow feather)

Mark and stitch pattern 181 in white. Stitch diagonal lines as shown, starting with the longest line in pink and continuing in rainbow order, to link the zigzag lines of *kaidan tsunagi*.

taka no hane
(hawk's feather)

Mark and stitch pattern 181 in white. Stitch diagonal lines as shown, starting with the longest line in pink and continuing in rainbow order. Note: short stitches start and finish in the centre of the grid squares.

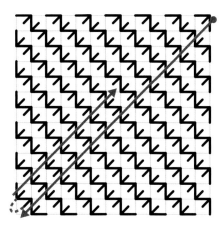
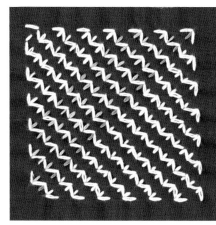

183

PATTERN TYPE: H C

jōkaku
(castellation)

Mark and stitch pattern 180 in white. Stitch vertical rows as shown, starting with pink and continuing in rainbow order, stranding across the back from one row to the next. Note: each vertical row is identical.

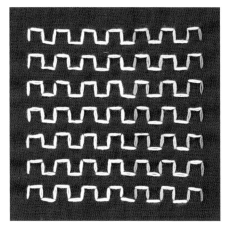
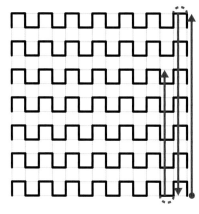

184

PATTERN TYPE: H C

yamagata
(mountain form)

Mark and stitch pattern 180 in white. Stitch vertical rows in rainbow order, starting with pink and peach lines at either side of the central stitches. Note: all other vertical rows are alternating.

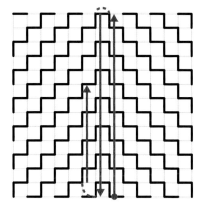

185

PATTERN TYPE: H C

Infinite Persimmon Flower

Repeating the central stitch rows creates many variations on the *kakinohanazashi* (persimmon flower stitch) motif. Starting rows with a stitch gives a central square; starting with a gap gives a cross.

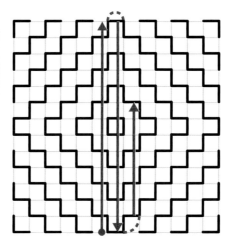

mugen kakinohanazashi
(infinite persimmon flower stitch)

Mark ¼in (6mm) grid, 13 x 13 squares. Stitch horizontal rows similar to pattern 180 but with two identical rows at the centre. Note: all other horizontal rows are alternating. Stitch vertical rows in rainbow order, starting with pink and peach lines at either side of the central stitches. Note: all other vertical rows are alternating.

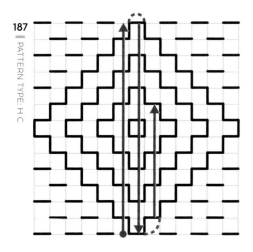

kawari mugen kakinohanazashi
(infinite persimmon flower stitch variation)

Mark ¼in (6mm) grid, 13 x 13 squares. Stitch horizontal rows as pattern 186. Stitch vertical rows, starting with pink and peach at either side of the central stitches. Continue in rainbow order. Towards the edge of the design, stitch only the vertical stitches as shown, so the motif floats on a background of horizontal stitches.

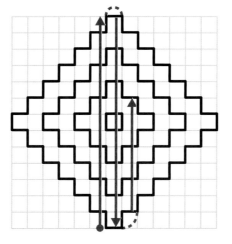

kawari mugen kakinohanazashi
(infinite persimmon flower stitch variation)

Mark ¼in (6mm) grid, 13 x 13 squares. Stitch horizontal rows in white, leaving part of the grid unstitched. Stitch vertical lines, starting with pink and peach at either side of the central square. Continue in rainbow order.

These patterns play with the basic flower motif, while the possibility for infinite expansion expresses a wish for increasing good fortune. When the second set of rows are added, the dramatic patterns are said to appear as if by magic. They can be extended into larger motifs for other projects.

kawari mugen kakinohanazashi
(infinite persimmon flower stitch variation)

Mark ¼in (6mm) grid, 13 x 13 squares. Stitch horizontal rows in white. Note: the first row starts with a gap, not a stitch. Stitch vertical rows, starting with pink and peach at either side of the central square. Continue in rainbow order.

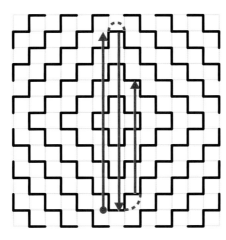

kawari mugen kakinohanazashi
(infinite persimmon flower stitch variation)

Mark ¼in (6mm) grid, 13 x 13 squares. Stitch horizontal rows in white as pattern 189. Stitch vertical rows, starting with pink and peach at either side of the central square. Continue in rainbow order.

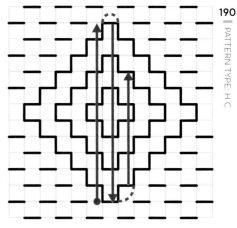

kawari mugen kakinohanazashi
(infinite persimmon flower stitch variation)

Mark ¼in (6mm) grid, 13 x 13 squares. Stitch horizontal rows in white, leaving part of the grid unstitched. Stitch vertical lines, starting with pink and peach at either side of the central square. Continue in rainbow order.

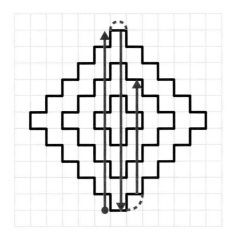

Persimmon Flower Patterns

Kakinohanazashi (persimmon flower stitch) patterns begin with a variation on *yokogushi* (horizontal rows) with repeated rows. The patterns appear as if by magic!

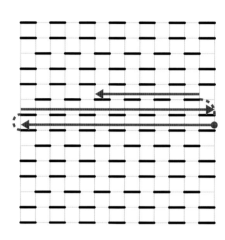

kawari yokogushi
(horizontal rows variation)

Mark ¼in (6mm) grid, 13 x 13 squares. Stitch horizontal lines in rainbow order, starting with identical pink and peach lines at the centre. Note: lines repeat in a 2 - 1 - 2 - 1 sequence (where '2' means two repeated lines and '1' means a single, alternating line).

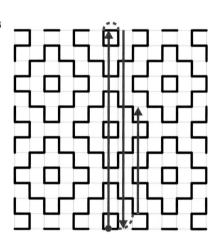

kakinohanazashi
(persimmon flower stitch)

Mark and stitch pattern 192 in white. Stitch vertical lines in rainbow order, starting with identical pink and peach lines at either side of the central stitches. Note: lines repeat in a 2 - 1 - 1 - 2 - 1 - 1 sequence.

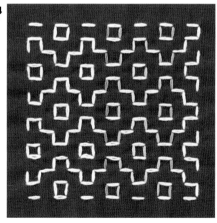

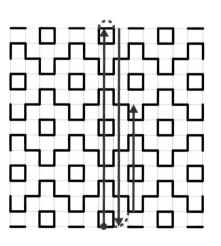

kakinohanazashi tsunagi
(linked persimmon flower stitch)

Mark and stitch pattern 192 in white. Stitch vertical lines in rainbow order, starting with identical pink and peach lines at either side of the central stitches. Note: lines repeat in a 2 - 2 - 2 sequence.

Kakinohanazashi *is one of the main patterns in the* hitomezashi *repertoire. In Shōnai, Yamagata Prefecture, it was used as a very hardwearing stitch on the shoulders and diagonal front bands of sorihikihappi (sledge-pulling waistcoats), and there was an element of competition over who could stitch the best example.*

mukai kakinohanazashi
(facing persimmon flower stitch)

Mark and stitch pattern 192 in white. Stitch vertical lines in rainbow order, starting with identical pink and peach lines at either side of the central stitches. Note: all other lines are alternating.

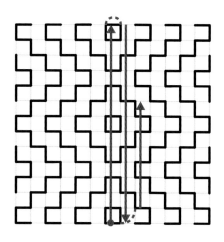

kakinohana to jūji
(persimmon flower and cross)

Mark and stitch pattern 192 in white. Stitch vertical lines in rainbow order, starting with identical pink and peach lines at either side of the central stitches. Note: lines repeat in a 2 - 1 - 2 - 2 - 1 sequence.

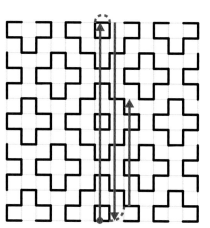

kakinohana to kōgoni jūji
(persimmon flower alternating with cross)

Mark and stitch pattern 192 in white. Stitch vertical lines in rainbow order, starting with identical pink and peach lines at either side of the central stitches. Note: lines repeat in a 2 - 1 - 2 - 1 - 2 sequence.

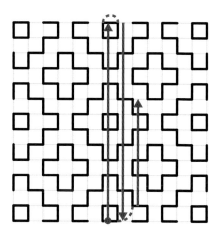

Mountains and Small Squares

Repeating identical foundation rows creates tiny squares and these are the basis for several other patterns that have a very modern look.

198

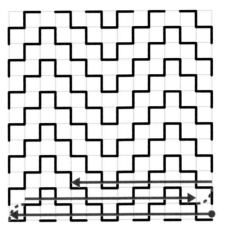

yamagata
(mountain form)

Mark and stitch pattern 192 as *vertical* rows in white. Stitch horizontal lines back and forth in rainbow order, starting from the bottom edge. Note: each horizontal row alternates with the previous one.

199

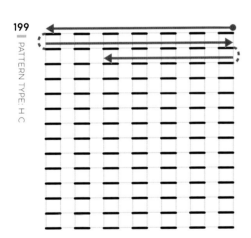

kawari yokogushi
(horizontal lines variation)

Mark ¼in (6mm) grid, 13 x 13 squares. Stitch horizontal rows back and forth in rainbow order, starting from the top edge. Note: each row is identical.

200

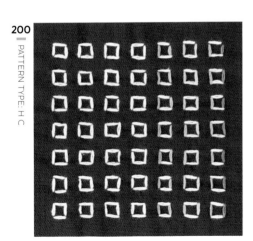
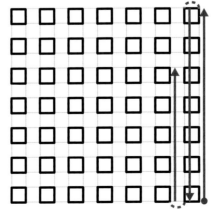

chiisana shikaku
(small squares)

Mark and stitch pattern 199 in white. Stitch vertical lines, starting with pink and continuing in rainbow order, linking the ends of the previous stitches to form small squares. Note: each vertical row is identical.

The stepped yamagata (mountain form) pattern and the small squares patterns that follow continue with the repeating rows as a starting point for the designs. Linking the small squares with diagonal stitches creates a miniature version of zenizashi patterns 170 and 171, with the same wish for wealth and prosperity.

zenizashi
(coin stitch)

Mark and stitch pattern 200 in white. Stitch the diagonal lines, starting with the longest line in pink and continuing in rainbow order, linking the corners of alternate squares.

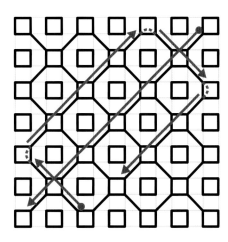

kaku tsunagi
(linked squares)

Mark and stitch pattern 200 in white. Stitch the diagonal lines, starting with the longest line in pink and continuing in rainbow order, linking the corners of the squares.

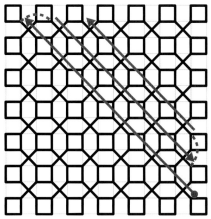

hon zenizashi
(true coin stitch)

Mark and stitch pattern 200 in white. Stitch the diagonal lines, starting with the longest line in pink and continuing in rainbow order, linking the squares. Note: the diagonal lines all cross the same way.

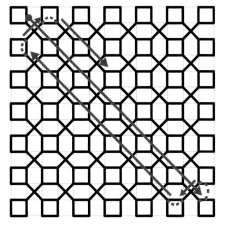

Steps, Crosses and Squares

Stitching the vertical foundation rows in pairs creates more possibilities, with patterns that include a smaller version of *yamagata* (mountain form) and designs that combine squares and crosses.

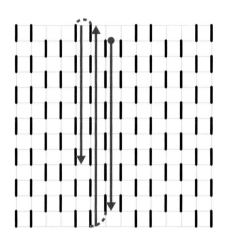

kawari tate kushi
(vertical line variation)

Mark ¼in (6mm) grid, 13 x 13 squares. Stitch pairs of vertical rows back and forth in rainbow order, starting with pink and peach at the centre and continuing with the rainbow order.

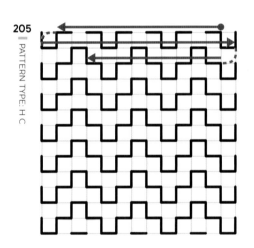

chiisana yamagata
(small mountain form)

Mark and stitch pattern 204 in white. Stitch horizontal lines back and forth in rainbow order, starting with pink and continuing in rainbow order. Note: each horizontal row alternates with the previous one.

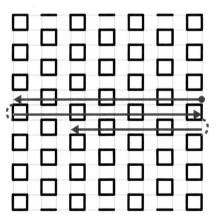

chiisana shikaku o kōgo ni
(alternating small squares)

Mark and stitch pattern 204 in white. Stitch horizontal lines, starting with pink and continuing in rainbow order, linking the ends of the previous stitches. Note: each horizontal row is identical.

Changing the placement of the repeated rows in hitomezashi *patterns brings possibilities for more than one pattern on the same foundation rows. Some antique* donza *(work kimono) have several patterns along the length of the front panels, an indication perhaps that their original makers enjoyed experimenting.*

---

jūji
(crosses)

Mark and stitch pattern 204 in white. Stitch horizontal lines, starting with pink and continuing in rainbow order. Note: lines repeat in a 2 - 1 - 2 - 1 sequence.

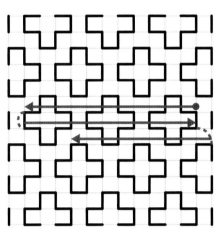
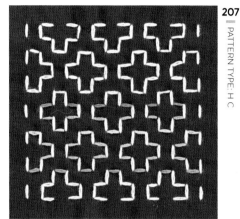

207

PATTERN TYPE: H C

---

kaku to jūji o kōgo ni
(alternating squares and crosses)

Mark and stitch pattern 204 in white. Stitch horizontal lines, starting with pink and continuing in rainbow order. Note: lines repeat in a 2 - 2 - 2 - 2 sequence.

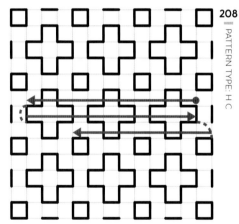

208

PATTERN TYPE: H C

---

kaku to jūji o kōgo ni tsunagi
(linked alternating squares and crosses)

Mark and stitch pattern 208 in white. Stitch diagonal lines, starting with the longest line in pink and continuing in rainbow order, linking the squares and crosses. (Note: the diagonal lines don't need to be marked as the stitches are lined up using the previously stitched pattern as a guide.)

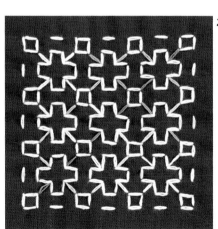

209

PATTERN TYPE: H C

83

Persimmon and Well Curb

Some *hitomezashi* (one stitch sashiko) patterns require specific sets of foundation rows that are unique to that pattern. These form interesting designs in their own right, although they are not usually stitched separately.

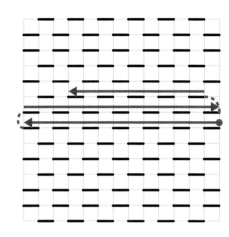

kawari yokogushi
(horizontal line variation)

Mark ¼in (6mm) grid, 13 x 13 squares. Stitch horizontal rows back and forth, starting with pink and continuing in rainbow order. Note: lines repeat in a 2 - 1 - 1 - 1 - 2 - 2 - 1 sequence.

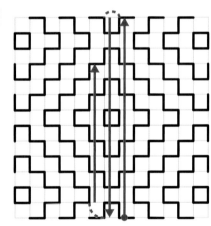

sanjū kakinohanazashi
(triple persimmon flower stitch)

Mark and stitch pattern 210 in white. Stitch vertical lines back and forth, starting with pink and continuing with the rainbow order. Note: all vertical lines are alternating rows apart from the central and side rows, which are in pairs.

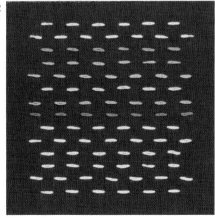

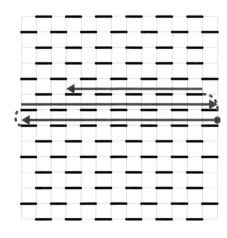

kawari yokogushi
(horizontal line variation)

Mark ¼in (6mm) grid, 13 x 13 squares. Stitch horizontal rows back and forth, starting with pink and continuing in rainbow order. Note: lines repeat in a 2 - 1 - 1 - 2 - 1 - 1 sequence.

These patterns need careful counting of the foundation rows to ensure that each one has the correct placement of stitches and gaps, or gaps and stitches. Traditional sashiko stitchers started with the simplest patterns and worked up to more challenging designs like these, placing stitches by eye without a grid!

kawari kakinohanazashi
(persimmon flower stitch variation)

Mark and stitch pattern 212 in white. Stitch vertical lines back and forth, starting with pink and continuing in rainbow order. Note: lines repeat in a 2 - 1 - 1 - 2 - 1 - 1 sequence.

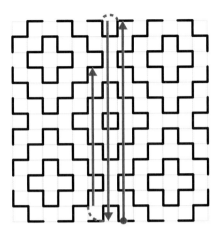

kawari yokogushi
(horizontal line variation)

Mark ¼in (6mm) grid, 13 x 13 squares. Stitch pairs of horizontal rows back and forth, starting with pink and continuing with the rainbow order. Note: carefully count the stitches and gaps as there are double gaps in some rows.

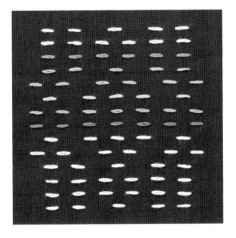
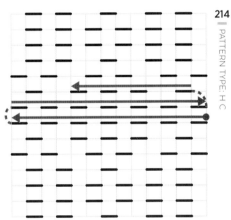

idowaku
(well frame)

Mark and stitch pattern 214 in white. Stitch vertical lines back and forth, starting with pink and continuing in rainbow order. Note: carefully count the stitches and gaps as there are double gaps in most rows.

Squares on Point

Turning a square through 45 degrees gives movement to a design. Some of the simpler ones work in different scales, such as *tatemimasu* (three upright square measures).

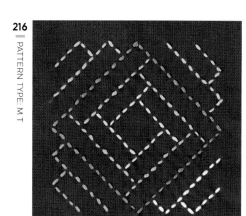

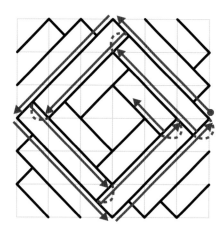

kumiko
(latticework)

Mark ½in (1.3cm) grid, 6 x 6 squares. Mark diagonal pattern lines as shown. Stitch the large square in pink, then continue to stitch in rainbow order, stranding across the back as shown.

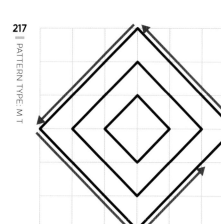

tatemimasu
(three upright square measures)

Mark ½in (1.3cm) grid, 6 x 6 squares. Mark diagonal pattern lines as shown. Stitch largest square in pink, then continue to stitch squares individually in rainbow order.

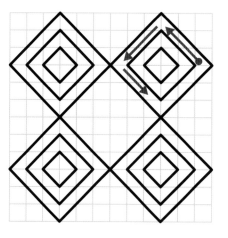

kawari tatemimasu
(three upright square measures variation)

Mark ¼in (6mm) grid, 12 x 12 squares. Mark diagonal pattern lines as shown. Stitch the overlapping diagonal rectangles as pattern 119, then stitch each of the smaller squares individually in rainbow order.

These patterns tessellate easily to create continuous designs for larger pieces of sashiko. Tatemimasu is usually spaced out with plain squares in a checkerboard effect. Turning kawari segaiha upside down and adding vertical lines turns it into matsuba and the pine tree, represented in the pattern by its needles, signifies long life.

kawari segaiha
(blue ocean wave variation)

Mark ½in (1.3cm) grid, 6 x 6 squares. Mark diagonal pattern lines as shown. Stitch the square on point in pink, then stitch the remaining lines in rainbow order, stranding across the back as shown.

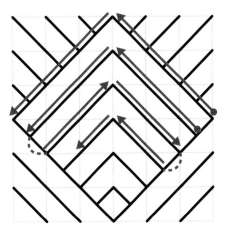 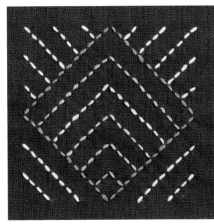

matsuba
(pine needle)

Mark as an upside down version of pattern 219. Stitch the vertical lines in pink, then stitch as upside down pattern 219 in white.

 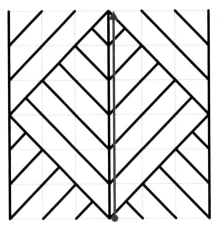

manji tsunagi shikaku mon
(linked manji square pattern)

Mark ¾in (2cm) grid, 4 x 4 squares. Mark diagonal pattern lines as shown. Stitch the small square on point in pink, then stitch the remaining lines individually in rainbow order.

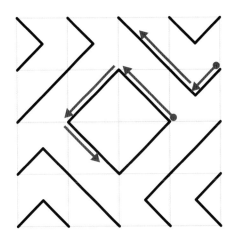 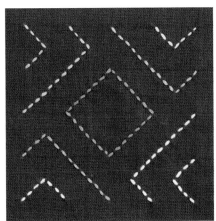

Stepped Patterns

Stepped or angled lines cross to create these easy patterns, which look like complex puzzles. Changing the scale slightly reveals more of the pattern.

222

PATTERN TYPE: M C

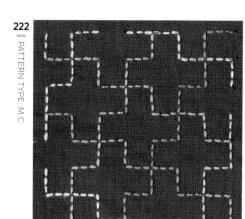

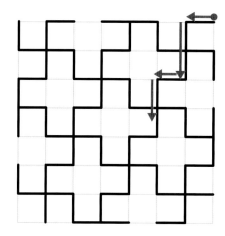

dan tsunagi
(linked steps)

Mark ½in (1.3cm) grid, 7 x 7 squares. Stitch the first stepped line in pink, then stitch the remaining lines individually in rainbow order.

223

PATTERN TYPE: M C

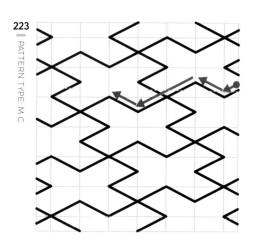

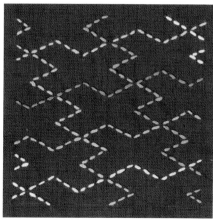

naname dan tsunagi
(diagonal linked steps)

Mark ½in (1.3cm) grid, 6 x 6 squares with a half square at each edge. Mark diagonal pattern lines as shown. Stitch the first stepped line in pink, then stitch the remaining lines individually in rainbow order.

224

PATTERN TYPE: M C

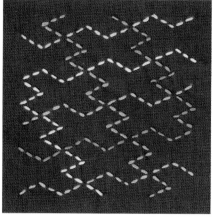

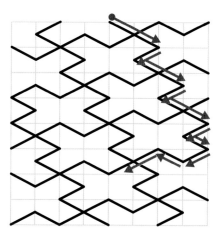

naname dan tsunagi
(diagonal linked steps)

Mark ⅜in (1cm) grid, 8 x 8 squares. Mark diagonal pattern lines as shown. Stitch the first stepped line in pink, then stitch the remaining lines individually in rainbow order.

The Buddhist manji symbol of the hooked cross originates in India, and represents the footsteps of Buddha, symbolising peace and prosperity. It forms the crossing point of these continuous sashiko lines, creating spaces rather like jigsaw pieces. Patterns 225 and 226 are from Hokusai's Shingata Komoncho (New Forms of Small Patterns).

kawari manji tsunagi
(linked manji variation)

Mark ⅜in (1cm) grid, 8 x 8 squares. Mark diagonal pattern lines as shown. Stitch the first stepped line in pink, then stitch the remaining lines individually in rainbow order.

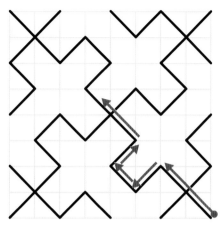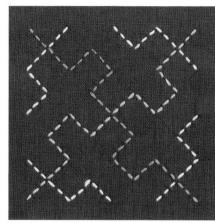

kawari manji tsunagi
(linked manji variation)

Mark ½in (1.3cm) grid, 6 x 6 squares. Mark diagonal pattern lines as shown. Stitch the first stepped line in pink, then stitch the remaining lines in peach and yellow.

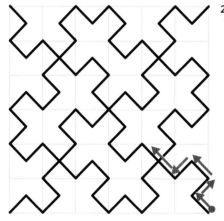

kawari manji tsunagi
(linked manji variation)

Mark ⅜in (1cm) grid, 8 x 8 squares. Mark diagonal pattern lines as shown. Stitch the first stepped line in pink, then stitch the remaining lines in rainbow order.

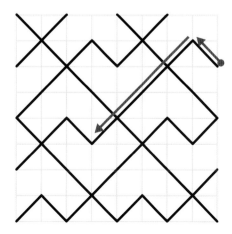

Diagonal Patterns

Manmade objects — bamboo fences, arrow feathers, octagonal *shōji* screen patterns — inspired these designs. Different parts of the *yamaji* (mountain road) pattern yields two blocks. Everyday things make elegant sashiko.

228

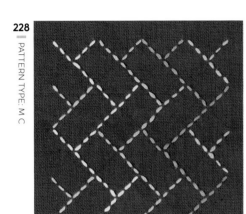
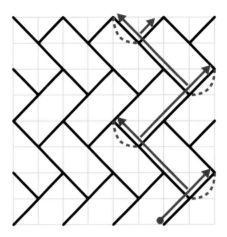

higaki
(cypress fence)

Mark ⅜in (1cm) grid, 8 x 8 squares. Mark diagonal pattern lines as shown. Stitch the first line in pink, then stitch the remaining lines individually in rainbow order, stranding across the back as shown.

229

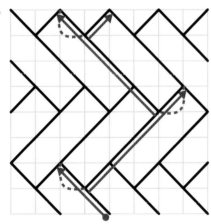

nagai higaki
(elongated cypress fence)

Mark ⅜in (1cm) grid, 8 x 8 squares. Mark diagonal pattern lines as shown. Stitch the first line in pink, then stitch the remaining lines individually in rainbow order, stranding across the back as shown.

230

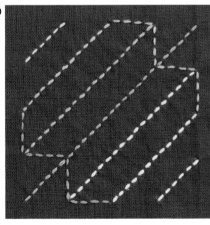
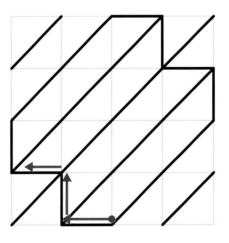

yabane
(arrow feather)

Mark ⅜in (1.3cm) grid, 8 x 8 squares. Mark diagonal pattern lines as shown. Stitch stepped lines in pink and peach first, then stitch the remaining lines individually in rainbow order.

Higaki (cypress fences) lend their woven pattern to damask kimono silk. Yabane (arrow feather) was originally a man's motif, but started to be used on wedding kimono during the Edo era (1603–1868), for good luck. The number eight is lucky, so the octagon is too, while Japan's mountainous landscape has many zigzag roads.

hakkaku yose
(gathered octagons)

Mark ½in (1.3cm) grid, 6 x 6 squares. Mark diagonal pattern lines as shown. Stitch the first line in pink, then stitch the remaining lines individually in rainbow order.

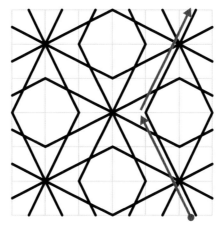

yamaji
(mountain road)

Mark ⅜in (1cm) grid, 8 x 8 squares. Mark diagonal pattern lines as shown. Stitch pattern 25 in white. Then stitch the zigzag lines in pink and peach.

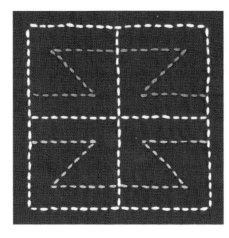
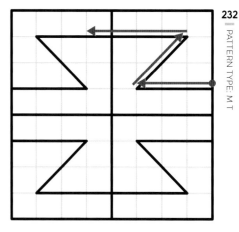

yamaji
(mountain road)

Mark ⅜in (1cm) grid, 8 x 8 squares. Mark diagonal pattern lines as shown. Stitch pattern 25 in white. Then stitch the zigzag lines in pink and peach.

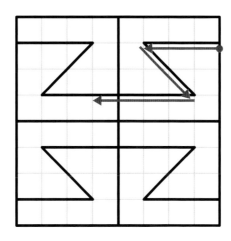
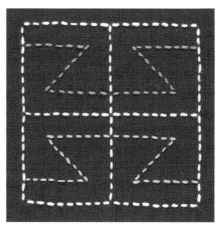

Grids and Diagonals

By adding various diagonal lines to pattern 25, the basic *koshi* (check), a variety of elaborate but easy to stitch patterns are made. These are all used for more elaborate *shōji* screens and *ranma* (transom panels).

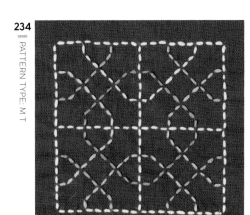

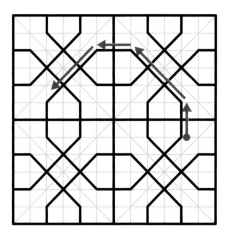

hakkaku tsunagi
(linked octagons)

Mark ¼in (6mm) grid, 12 x 12 squares. Mark the blue diagonals as guidelines only (these are not stitched), and the stitching lines in black. Stitch pattern 25 in white. Stitch the centre octagon in pink, and remaining lines individually in rainbow order.

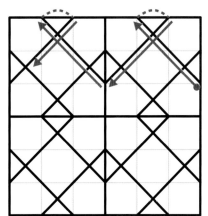

hiyoku igeta
(paired well curb)

Mark ½in (1.3cm) grid, 6 x 6 squares. Mark diagonal pattern lines, lined up on the grid. Stitch centre square on point in pink, then stitch remaining lines in rainbow order, stranding across the back as shown.

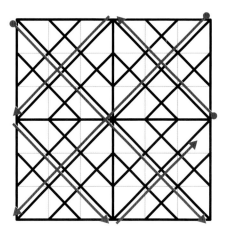

kasane masu tsunagi
(layered linked square measures)

Mark pattern 28 and mark additional diagonal lines from pattern 235. Stitch pattern 28 in white, then stitch the remaining (rainbow order) lines from pattern 235 in pink.

Masu, the square measuring boxes that give their name to several sashiko patterns, are stacking wooden boxes that were once used as rice measures. Yatsude asanoha is the fatsia japonica *plant, planted outside many homes for good luck. The character for the number eight (*hachi*) can also mean infinite or expansive.*

yatsude asanoha
(eight lobed hemp leaf)

Mark ⅜in (1cm) grid, 8 x 8 squares. Mark diagonal pattern lines as shown. Stitch pattern 28 in white. Stitch first shallow zigzag line in pink, the second in peach and the others in white. Stitch horizontal and vertical short lines in rainbow order, stranding across the back.

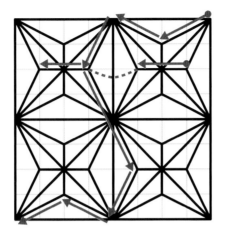

kawari yatsude asanoha
(eight lobed hemp leaf variation)

Mark pattern 237, but omitting some shallow zigzags and short horizontal and vertical lines. Stitch pattern 28 in white. Stitch first shallow zigzag line in pink, and the second in peach. Stitch short lines individually continuing in rainbow order.

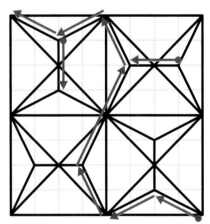

chōchin masu tsunagi
(linked square measure lanterns)

Mark ⅜in (1cm) grid, 8 x 8 squares. Mark diagonal pattern lines as shown. Stitch pattern 25 in white. Then stitch small squares on point individually in pink. Stitch horizontal and vertical lines in rainbow order, stranding across the back.

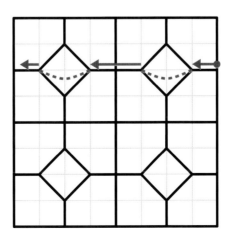
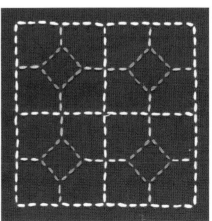

Key and Fret Patterns

Key patterns are easy to draw and stitch, while the fret designs focus on different areas to create two blocks from one pattern, including an optical illusion of weaving.

240

PATTERN TYPE: M C

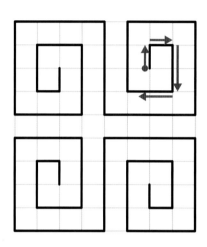

tsunagi raimon
(linked square lightning spiral)

Mark ⅜in (1cm) grid, 9 x 8 squares. Stitch the pink double spiral, followed by the peach double spiral.

241

PATTERN TYPE: M T

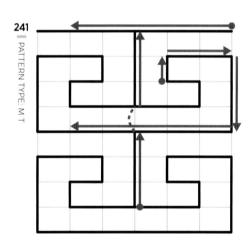

sayagata kuzushi
(cursive sayagata)

Mark ⅜in x ½in (1cm x 1.3cm) grid, 8 x 6 rectangles. Stitch the pink horizontal line first, then stitch the two pattern sections in peach and yellow. Stitch the green vertical line, stranding across the back as shown.

242

PATTERN TYPE: M T

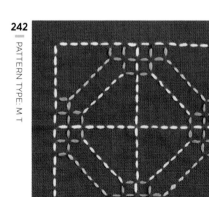

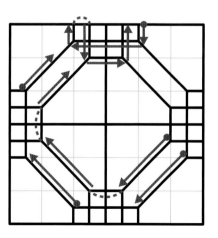

futate kaku shokkō
(double angle shokkō brocade)

Mark ½in (1.3cm) grid, 6 x 6 squares, plus additional ¼in (6mm) lines in the two squares at the midpoint of each side. Mark diagonal pattern lines as shown. Stitch pattern 25 in white. Stitch the small grilles in pink. Stitch the diagonal lines, stitching peach lines individually and yellow lines by stranding across the back as shown.

Raimon, *the square spiral, indicates lightning and represents* Raijin, *the protective god of thunder, also known as Kaminari-sama. Shokkō patterns are based on a luxurious imported Chinese brocade. The doubled lines of* kawari kakuyose *symbolise strength.*

futate kaku shokkō
(double angle shokkō brocade)

Mark ½in (1.3cm) grid, 6 x 6 squares, plus additional ¼in (6mm) lines in the corner squares and the four central squares. Mark the diagonal pattern lines as shown. Stitch pattern 25 in white. Stitch the small grilles in pink. Stitch the diagonals in rainbow order, stopping and restarting at either side of the central grille.

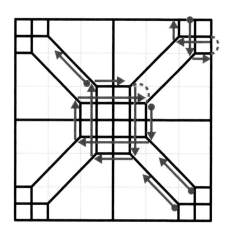

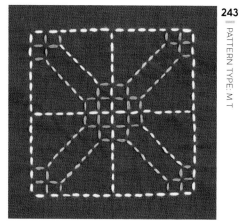

kawari kakuyose
(intersecting square corners variation)

Mark ½in (1.3cm) grid, 6 x 6 squares. Mark pattern lines ⅛in (3mm) from the grid lines as shown. Stitch in rainbow order, stranding across the back to make the woven effect.

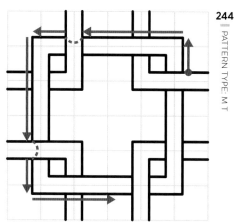

kawari kakuyose
(intersecting square corners variation)

Mark ½in (1.3cm) grid, 6 x 6 squares. Mark pattern lines ⅛in (3mm) from the grid lines as shown. Stitch in rainbow order, stranding across the back to make the woven effect.

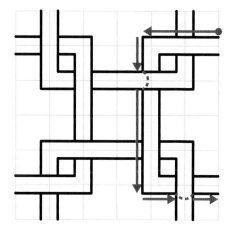

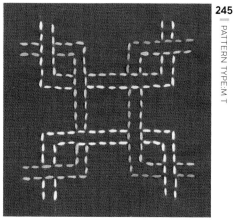

Hexagons

Hexagons in Japanese design are often drawn over a square grid rather than having true 60-degree angles, making these designs easy to mark as well as stitch.

246

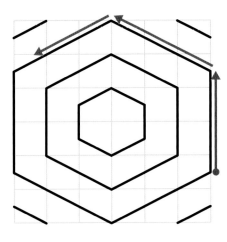

kikkō
(hexagon)

Mark ½in (1.3cm) grid, 6 x 6 squares. Mark diagonal pattern lines as shown. Stitch hexagons individually, starting with the largest in pink, and continuing in rainbow order.

247

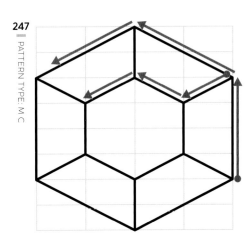

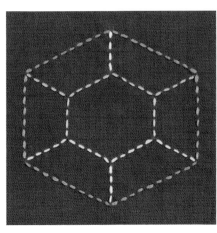

arare kikkō
(hailstone hexagon)

Mark ⅜in x ¾in (1cm x 2cm) grid, 8 x 4 rectangles. Mark diagonal pattern lines as shown. Stitch large hexagon outline in pink, then stitch peach and yellow zigzags and short vertical lines individually.

248

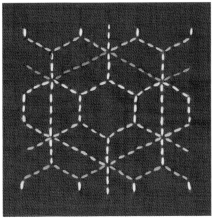

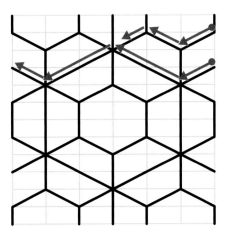

arare kikkō
(hailstone hexagons)

Mark ¼in x ½in (6mm x 1.3cm) grid, 12 x 6 rectangles. Mark diagonal pattern lines as shown. Stitch first large zigzag in pink. Stitch remaining zigzags in rainbow order. Then stitch vertical lines in white, stranding across the back.

As described in Weaves and Crosses, hexagons are named after the turtle's shell and represent a wish for long life. The turtle is often depicted alongside the crane, a bird said to live for a thousand years, while the turtle lives ten times longer! The turtle is represented only by its shell, perhaps because it is not as graceful as the crane!

kasane kikkō
(layered hexagons)

Mark ⅜in x ¾in (1cm x 2cm) grid, 8 x 4 rectangles. Mark diagonal pattern lines as shown. Stitch large zigzag in pink. Stitch remaining zigzags in rainbow order. Stitch vertical lines last, stranding across the back.

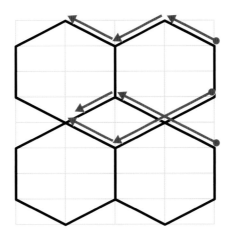
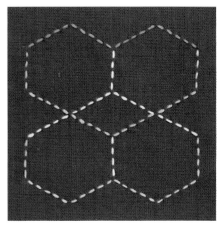

kumo no su kikkō
(spider's web hexagon)

Mark ⅜in grid, 8 x 8 squares. Mark diagonal pattern lines as shown. Stitch large hexagon in pink, then stitch the smaller hexagons in rainbow order, adding the lines across the hexagon and corners last.

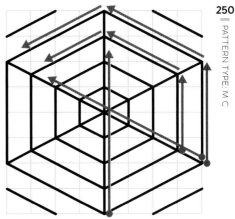

matsuba kikkō
(pine needle hexagon)

Mark ⅜in (1cm) grid, 8 x 8 squares. Mark diagonal pattern lines as shown. Stitch large hexagon and vertical line in pink. Stitch remaining lines in rainbow order, back and forth across the hexagon, stranding across the back from one line to the next.

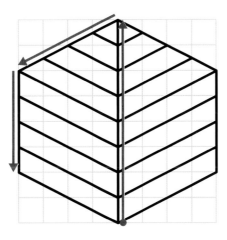
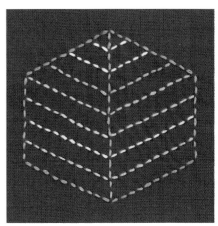

Linked Hexagons

Many patterns use linked hexagons as a starting point for continuous designs. Pattern 252 *kikkō* (hexagon) is shared as the foundation, marked on square grids.

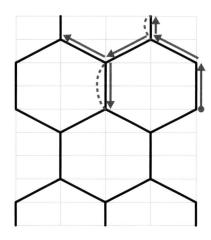

kikkō
(hexagon)

Mark ⅜in x ¾in (1cm x 2cm) grid, 9 x 4 rectangles. Mark diagonal pattern lines as shown. Stitch top hexagon section in pink, stranding across the back to stitch verticals, and continue in rainbow order.

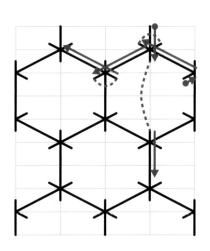
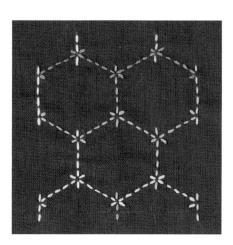

tsuno kikkō
(horned hexagon)

Mark pattern 252. Stitch top line of top hexagon section in pink, stranding across the back to cross corners, and continue in rainbow order. Stitch verticals, crossing corners and stranding across the back.

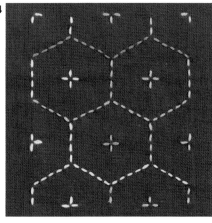
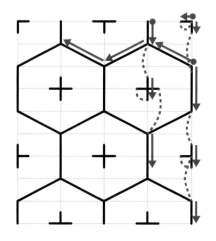

jūji kikkō
(cross hexagons)

Mark pattern 252. Stitch zigzags in pink, peach and yellow. Stitch vertical lines in rainbow order, stranding across the back, stitching the central crosses back and forth in each hexagon.

Because the hexagon pattern is associated with longevity, it has been used to decorate all kinds of objects and materials. The shape lends itself to being filled in with various other patterns, so there is a lot of variety to kikkō designs, many of which date back to ancient times.

hiyoku kikkō
(layered hexagons)

Mark ⅜in (1cm) grid, 9 x 8 squares. Mark diagonal pattern lines as shown. Stitch pattern 252 in white. Stitch half hexagons in pink, stranding across the back. Stitch small hexagons individually, in rainbow order.

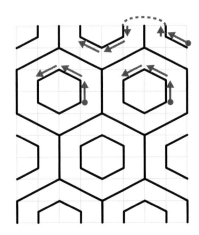
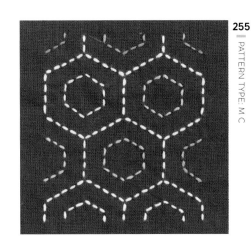

hoshi kikkō
(star hexagon)

Mark pattern 252, extending lines across hexagons to make stars. Stitch vertical lines first in rainbow order, stranding across the back, then stitch diagonal lines as shown.

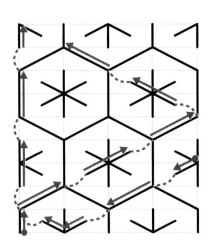

musubi kasane kikkō
(layered hexagon knot)

Mark pattern 252. Mark additional pattern lines. Stitch pattern 252 in white. Stitch remaining lines in rainbow order, back and forth, stranding across the back as shown.

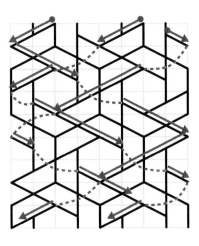
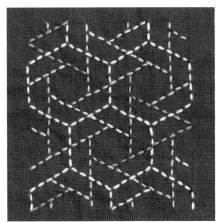

Gentian Flower

Delicately arranged lines fanning out from a central point are a feature of *rindō* (gentian) flower designs, which work on a hexagonal or diamond foundation.

PATTERN TYPE: M C

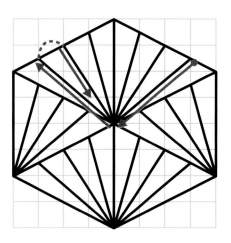

rindō hishi
(gentian diamond)

Mark ⅜in (1cm) grid, 8 x 8 squares. Mark diagonal pattern lines as shown. Stitch hexagon outline and lines that cross the hexagon in white. Stitch fanned lines in rainbow order, stranding across the back as shown.

259

PATTERN TYPE: M C

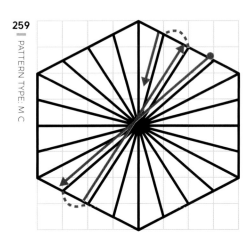

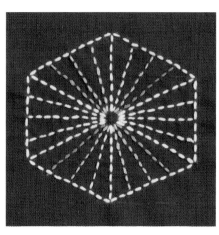

rindō
(gentian)

Mark ⅜in (1cm) grid, 8 x 8 squares. Mark diagonal pattern lines as shown. Stitch the hexagon outline in white. Stitch fanned lines in rainbow order, stranding across the back as shown.

260

PATTERN TYPE: M T

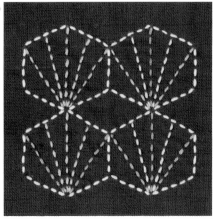

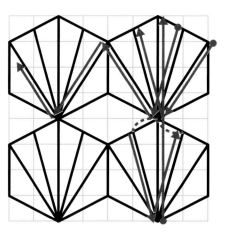

tsunagi rindō kikkō to hishi
(linked gentian hexagons and diamonds)

Mark ⅜in (1cm) grid, 8 x 8 squares. Mark diagonal pattern lines as shown. Stitch pattern 249 in white. Stitch fanned lines in rainbow order, stranding across the back as shown.

Rindō *designs are all popular if sophisticated* kumiko *(latticework)*
patterns, more often used as an openwork design rather than a
papered shōji *screen. The gentian flower is associated with autumn,*
when it is in bloom, and this motif dates from the Heian era (794–
*1185*CE*) when noblemen favoured it as a textile pattern.*

tsunagi rindō kikkō
(linked gentian hexagons)

Mark ⅜in (1cm) grid, 9 x 8 squares. Mark
the diagonal pattern lines as shown. Stitch
vertical lines and hexagon zigzags in white.
Stitch diagonal zigzags in pink and peach.
Stitch fanned lines vertically in rainbow
order, stranding across the back as shown.

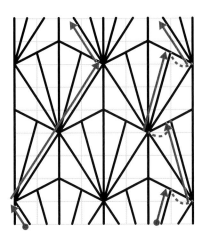

rindō tsunagi
(linked gentian)

Mark ¾in x ½in (2cm x 1.3cm) grid, 4 x 6
rectangles. Mark the diagonal pattern lines
as shown. Stitch hexagon outline in pink.
Stitch remaining lines in rainbow order.

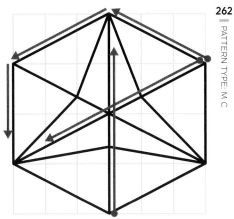

kasane rindō
(layered gentian)

Mark pattern 262. Mark a second 'triangle'
upside down inside the hexagon. Stitch
pattern 262 in white. Stitch the second
'triangle' in pink.

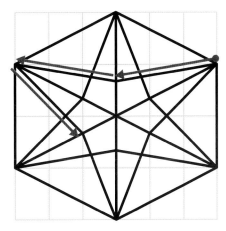

Layered Hexagons

Overlapping hexagons create attractive designs that are easy to stitch. More elaborate patterns include *karabana* (a mythical flower) and *daria* (dahlia).

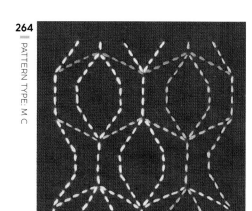

264

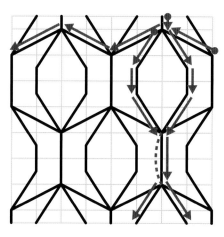

niiju kikkō tsunagi
(double linked hexagons)

Mark ⅜in (1cm) grid, 7 x 8 squares, with a half square at top and bottom. Mark diagonal pattern lines as shown. Stitch horizontal zigzags in rainbow order (pink, peach, yellow). Stitch vertical lines continuing with rainbow order (green, blue lilac), stranding across the back as required.

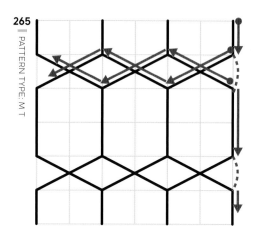

265

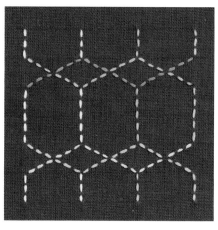

kasane kikkō
(layered hexagons)

Mark ½in (1.3cm) grid, 6 x 6 squares. Mark diagonal pattern lines as shown. Stitch horizontal zigzags in rainbow order (pink, peach, yellow, green). Stitch vertical lines continuing with rainbow order (blue, lilac), stranding across the back as required.

266

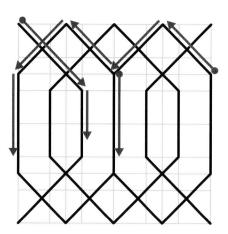

yae kikkō
(eight layer hexagons)

Mark ½in (1.3cm) grid, 6 x 6 squares, plus additional lines ¾in (2cm) in from all sides. Mark diagonal pattern lines as shown. Stitch lines following the rainbow order, starting with pink.

Karabana, *an imaginary flower from China, appeared in Japan during the Heian era (794–1185CE). Used for many* kamon *(family crest) designs, it usually has four petals but may have five or even six. The dahlia (*daria*) flower was introduced to Japan in the Meiji era (1868–1912CE) and* daria kikkō *is a variant on* rindō *(pattern 259).*

tsunagi karabana kikkō
(linked karabana flower hexagons)

Mark ½in (1.3cm) grid, 6x 6 squares, with additional horizontal lines ¼in (6mm) apart. Mark diagonal pattern lines as shown. Stitch around flower outline in pink. Stitch remaining lines in rainbow order. Stitch long diagonals in white.

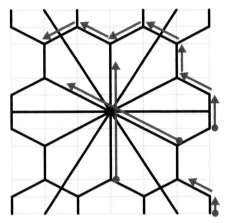
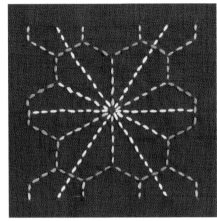

karabana kikkō
(karabana flower hexagon)

Mark 1⅝in x 1¾in (4cm x 4.5cm) grid, 2 x 2 rectangles. Mark 60° diagonal pattern lines as shown. Note: flower measures 1¼in (3cm) along shortest lines from centre. Stitch around flower outline in pink. Stitch remaining lines in rainbow order.

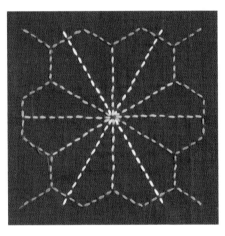
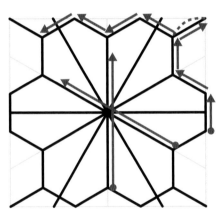

daria kikkō
(dahlia hexagon)

Mark pattern 259. Draw 2⅜in (6cm), 1½in (4cm) and 1⅛in (3cm) circles centred on the pattern and use these to mark short lines and zigags as shown. Stitch hexagon outline in pink, outer 'circle' in peach, and inner zigzags in yellow. Stitch radiating lines in rainbow order, stranding across the back as shown.

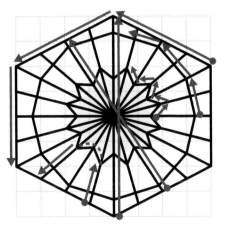

Linked Diamonds and Mountains

Connected diamonds make several different patterns when extra lines are added, and there's yet another *yamagata* (mountain form) pattern plus variation.

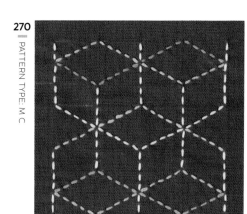

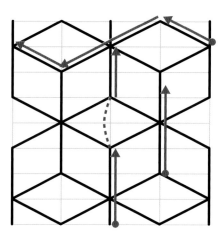

hakozashi
(box stitch)

Mark ⅜in x ¾in (1cm x 2cm) grid, 8 x 4 rectangles. Mark diagonal pattern lines. Stitch the horizontal zigzags, starting with pink and continuing in rainbow order. Stitch vertical lines in white, stranding across the back as required.

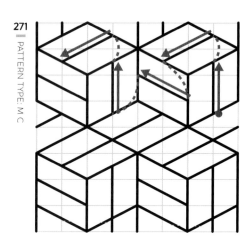

yosegi
(parquetry)

Mark ⅜in (1cm) grid, 8 x 8 squares. Mark diagonal pattern lines. Stitch pattern 270 in white. Stitch additional diagonal lines, starting with pink and continuing in rainbow order, stranding across the back as required.

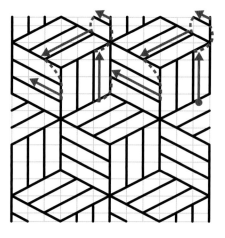

kawari yosegi
(parquetry variation)

Mark ¼in (6mm) grid, 11 x 12 squares, plus additional lines ⅛in (3mm) in from top and bottom. Mark diagonal pattern lines as shown. Stitch pattern 270 in white. Stitch additional lines starting with pink and continuing in rainbow order, stranding across the back as required.

Yosegi *(parquetry)* patterns combine diamonds *(for increase and prosperity)* with hexagons *(for long life)*, so these are extra lucky designs. In Japan, mountains are considered to be the homes of kami, the deities and spirits of the Shinto religion, so mountain designs have a spiritual dimension.

kawari asanoha
(hemp leaf variation)

Mark pattern 270. Mark additional diagonal and horizontal pattern lines as shown. Stitch pattern 270 in white. Stitch additional lines in rainbow order.

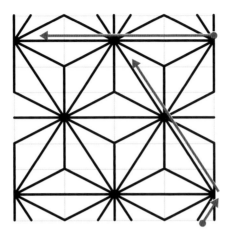

yamagata
(mountain form)

Mark ⅜in (1cm) grid, 8 x 8 squares. Mark diagonal pattern lines as shown. Stitch lines in rainbow order, starting with pink, stranding across the back on the last row.

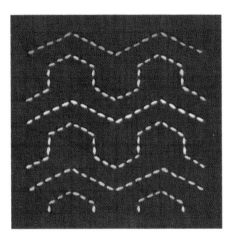

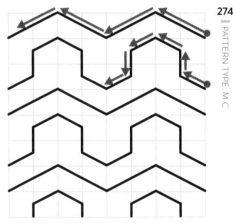

mukai kikkō
(alternate hexagons)

Mark and stitch pattern 274 in white. Stitch vertical lines in rainbow order, stranding across the back as shown.

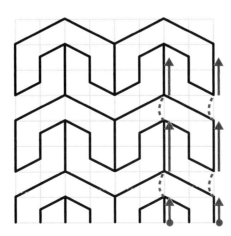

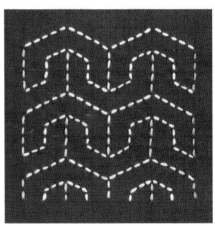

Bishamon Patterns

Bishamon, the Buddhist guardian of the north, is one of the Seven Gods of Good Luck. His armour scales have many patterns, mainly based on three hexagons.

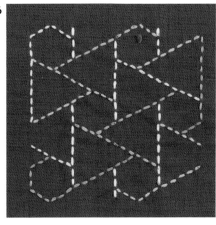

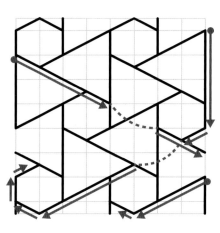

musubi kikkō
(knotted hexagons)

Mark ⅜in (1cm) grid, 7 x 8 squares, plus additional lines ³⁄₁₆in (5mm) in from top and bottom. Mark diagonal pattern lines as shown. Stitch lines in rainbow order, stranding across the back as required.

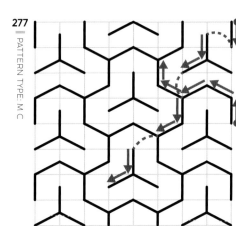

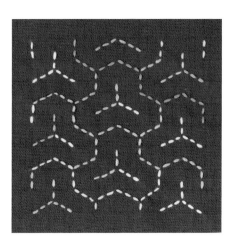

bishamon
(Bishamon armour scale pattern)

Mark ⅜in (1cm) grid, 8 x 8 squares. Mark diagonal pattern lines as shown. Stitch the pink, peach and yellow lines first and continue in rainbow order, starting with green, stranding across the back as required (note: stitching of pink and green lines are shown on the diagram).

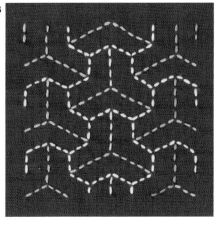

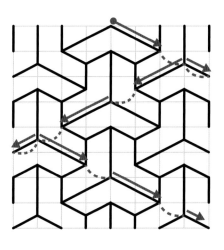

bishamon ken
(Bishamon sword)

Mark in similar way to pattern 277, but extending the triple centre lines. Stitch the triple hexagon outlines in white. Stitch additional lines starting with pink, peach and yellow vertical lines, stranding across the back as shown, and continuing in rainbow order, stranding across the back as required.

These patterns all confer the protection of Bishamon. *Not only is he one of the four heavenly kings that protect the world, but he is also the god of wealth, protecting riches, and therefore depicted wearing ornate armour. Kawari mukai kikkō, pattern 281, is taken from an antique* furoshiki *(wrapping cloth) in my collection.*

maru bishamon
(circular Bishamon)

Mark vertical lines 1½in (4cm) apart. Mark diagonal lines at a 60° angle, starting from the centre, and overlapping 2⅜in (6cm) circles. Stitch lines in rainbow order, stranding across the back as required.

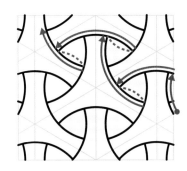

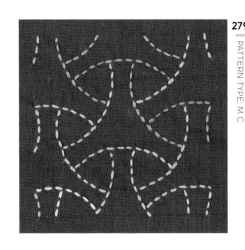

279

PATTERN TYPE: M C

kawari bishamon
(Bishamon variation)

Mark ⅜in (1cm) grid, 8 x 8 squares. Mark diagonal pattern lines as shown. Stitch lines in rainbow order, starting with pink, stranding across the back as required.

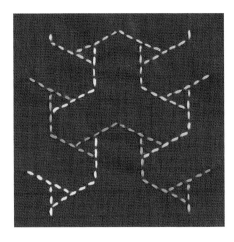

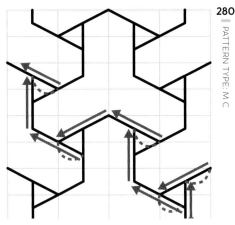

280

PATTERN TYPE: M C

kawari mukai kikkō
(alternate hexagons variation)

Mark ¼in (6mm) vertical lines, and horizontal lines ¼in (6mm) and ¾in (2cm) apart at the top, centre and bottom. Mark diagonal pattern lines as shown. Stitch lines in rainbow order, stranding across the back as shown.

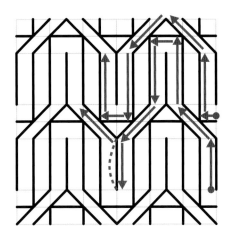

281

PATTERN TYPE: M C

Hexagonal Basketweaves

Bamboo baskets inspire several patterns creating woven effects. All drawn on diagonal grids, they lead into other patterns drawn on a 1:2 ratio rectangle.

282

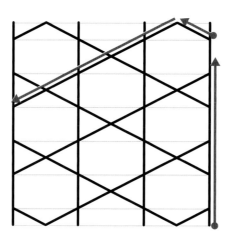

kagome
(bamboo basket)

Mark ½in x 1in (1.3cm x 1cm) grid, 5 x 3 rectangles, with a half square at top and bottom. Mark diagonal pattern lines as shown. Stitch lines in rainbow order, starting with vertical lines in pink, peach, yellow and green.

283

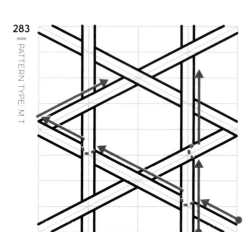

niiju kagome
(double bamboo basket)

Mark ⅜in x ¾in (1cm x 2cm) grid, 8 x 4 rectangles. Mark diagonal lines on the grid as shown. Mark pattern lines ⅛in (3mm) at either side of grid lines as shown. Note the woven effect, where one line overlaps another. Stitch lines in rainbow order, stranding across the back as required.

284

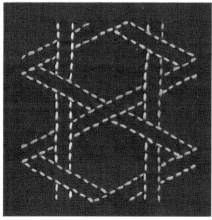
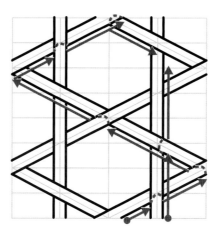

niiju kagome
(double bamboo basket)

Mark ⅜in x ¾in (1cm x 2cm) grid, 8 x 4 rectangles. Mark diagonal lines on the grid as shown. Mark pattern lines ⅛in (3mm) at either side of grid lines as shown. Note the woven effect, where one line overlaps another. Stitch in rainbow order, stranding across the back as required.

Kagome is made up of two words, 'kago' (basket) and 'me' (eye), so the focus is very much on the gaps in the weave forming the pattern. It is a protective pattern, forming a fence against misfortune. Kawari bishamon kikkō has elements of kagome and bishamon patterns.

sankaku
(triangles)

Mark ¾in x 1½in (2cm x 4cm) grid, 4 x 2 rectangles. Mark diagonal pattern lines as shown. Stitch lines in rainbow order.

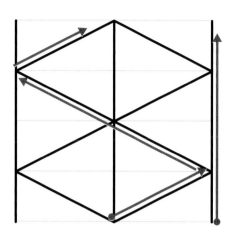

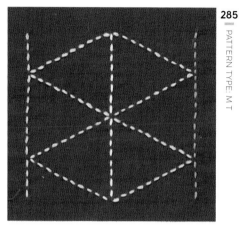

hishi asanoha
(diamond hemp leaf)

Mark ¾in x 1½in grid (2cm x 4cm), 4 x 2 rectangles. Mark vertical lines ⅜in (1cm) at either side of central vertical. Mark diagonal pattern lines as shown. Stitch lines in rainbow order, stranding across the back as required.

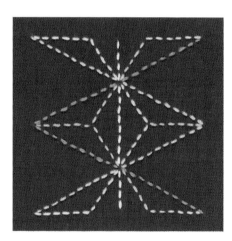

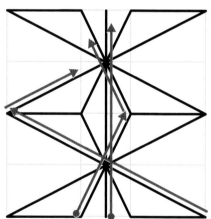

kawari bishamon kikkō
(Bishamon hexagons variation)

Mark ⅜in (1cm) grid, 8 x 8 squares. Mark diagonal pattern lines as shown. Stitch lines in rainbow order, stranding across the back as shown.

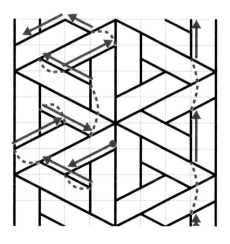

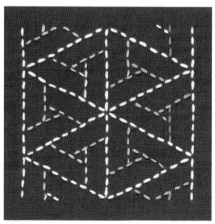

Diamonds

Overlapping diamond shapes in various ways creates many different patterns, all easy to stitch. These designs are often used for *shōji* and *ranma* screens.

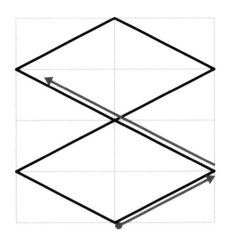

hishi
(diamond)

Mark ¾in x 1½in (2cm x 4cm) grid, 4 x 2 rectangles. Mark diagonal pattern lines as shown. Stitch diagonal lines in a continuous figure of eight, starting with pink, followed by peach.

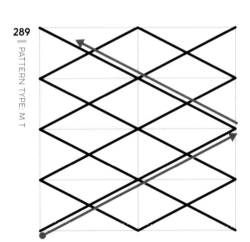

hishi moyō
(diamond pattern)

Mark ¾in x 1½in (2cm x 4cm) grid, 4 x 2 rectangles. Mark diagonal pattern lines as shown. Stitch pattern 288 in white, then stitch two sideways V-shapes individually in pink and peach.

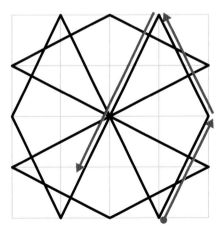

kasanebishi
(layered diamonds)

Mark ¾in (2cm) grid, 4 x 4 squares. Mark diagonal pattern lines as shown. Stitch two overlapping figures of eight, as in pattern 288, in rainbow order.

miebishi
(triple diamonds)

Mark ¾in x ½in (2cm x 1.3cm) grid , 4 x 6 rectangles. Mark pattern 288. Mark additional parallel diagonal lines as shown. Stitch pattern 288 in white. Stitch asymmetrical figures of eight in pink and peach.

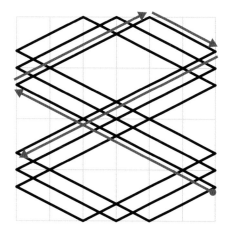 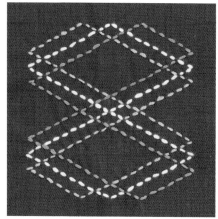

291

PATTERN TYPE: M T

hishi igeta
(diamond well curb)

Mark ⅜in grid (1cm), 9 x 8 rectangles. Mark diagonal pattern lines as shown. Stitch lines in rainbow order, stranding across the back as required.

 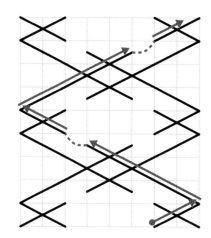

292

PATTERN TYPE: M C

ajiro waribishi
(wickerwork divided diamonds)

Mark ¾in x ½in (2cm x 1.3cm) grid , 4 x 6 rectangles. Mark pattern 288. Mark additional parallel diagonal lines as shown. Stitch pattern 288 in white. Stitch lines in rainbow order.

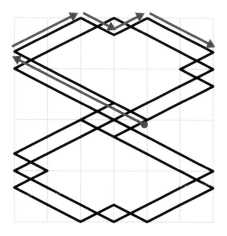 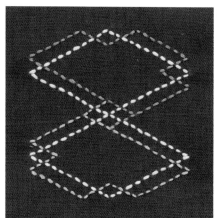

293

PATTERN TYPE: M T

More Diamonds

Changing the diamond infill makes more variations. Overlapping the diamond zigzags creates *matsukawabishi* (pine bark diamond), a famous pattern.

294

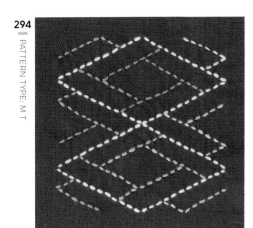

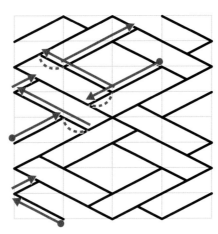

hishi manji
(diamond Buddhist manji)

Mark ⅜in x ¾in (2cm x 4cm) grid, 4 x 3 rectangles. Mark diagonal pattern lines as shown. Stitch 288 in white. Stitch each *manji* motif, starting with pink and continuing in rainbow order, stranding across the back as required.

295

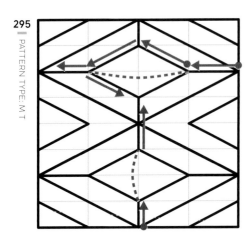

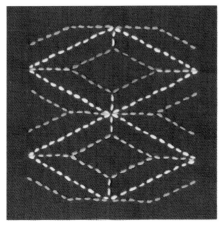

sanjū hishi tsunagi
(three linked diamonds)

Mark ⅜in x ¾in (1cm x 2cm) grid, 8 x 4 rectangles. Mark the diagonal pattern lines as shown. Stitch pattern 288 in white. Stitch remaining lines in rainbow order, stranding across the back as required. The final lilac lines may be stitched individually, as on the sample, or as a continuous outline as shown on the diagram.

296

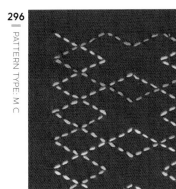

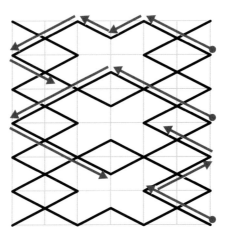

yotsugumi hishi
(quadruple diamonds)

Mark ½in (1.3cm) grid, 6 x 6 squares. Mark diagonal pattern lines on grid. Stitch diamonds individually in rainbow order, finishing with the zigzag verticals in green and blue.

Diamonds crossed with the Buddhist manji *or the well curb pattern are both beautiful and auspicious designs. The pine tree, with its association with long life, is referenced once again in the* matsukawabishi *designs. These patterns are found on many objects and materials in Japan.*

idowaku
(diagonal well curb)

Mark ⅜in x ⁵⁄₁₆in (1cm x 8mm) grid, 9 x 10 squares. Mark the diagonal pattern lines as shown, lining up your ruler with the grid. Stitch each well curb motif individually, starting with pink and continuing in rainbow order.

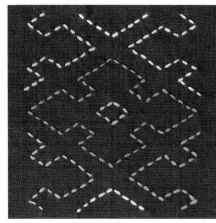

matsukawabishi
(pine bark diamond)

Mark ⅜in grid (1cm), 8 x 8 squares. Mark the diagonal pattern lines as shown, lining up your ruler with the grid. Stitch lines in rainbow order.

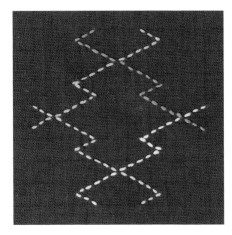
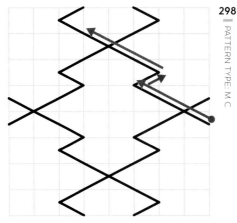

hishi matsukawabishi
(diamond with pine bark diamond)

Mark ⅜in (1cm) grid, 8 x 10 squares. Mark the diagonal pattern lines as shown, lining up your ruler with the grid. Stitch lines in rainbow order, starting with pink.

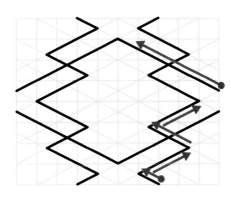
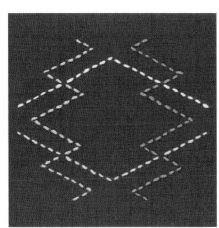

Weaves and Waves

These intriguing woven patterns on diamond grids are easier than they look. Diamonds make *segaiha* (blue ocean wave) and *matsuba* (pine needle) more elegant too.

300

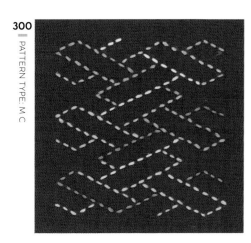
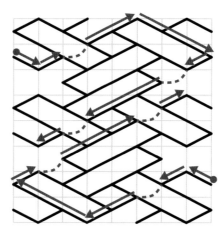

kumi hishi
(interlaced diamonds)

Mark ⅜in (1cm) grid, 8 x 8 squares. Mark the diagonal pattern lines. Stitch in pink, following the line around the pattern, stranding across the back as required. Continue in rainbow order.

301

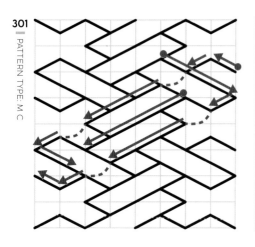
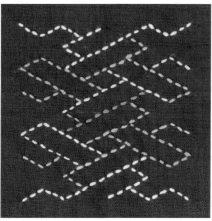

kumi hishi
(interlaced diamonds)

Mark ⅜in (1cm) grid, 8 x 8 squares. Mark the diagonal pattern lines. Stitch the short central pink line first, then continue to stitch lines around the pattern in rainbow order, stranding across the back as required.

302

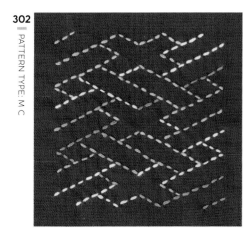
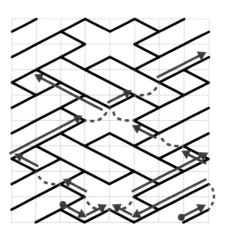

kumi hishi
(interlaced diamonds)

Mark ⅜in (1cm) grid, 8 x 8 squares. Mark the diagonal pattern lines. Stitch in pink, following the line around the pattern, stranding across the back as required. Continue in rainbow order.

The three kumi hishi *blocks are a good example of how centring on different areas of a larger continuous pattern can create several small sashiko samples. As a larger sample, it would be stitched with continuous straight lines, stranding across the back.*

ajiro manji
(diagonal well curb)

Mark ⅜in (1cm) grid, 8 x 8 squares. Mark the diagonal pattern lines as shown. Stitch pattern 288 in white, then stitch lines in rainbow order, starting with pink.

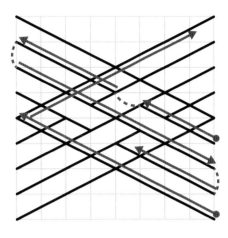
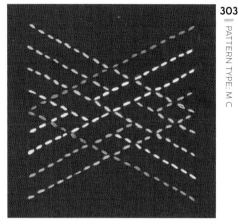

303

PATTERN TYPE: M C

hishi seigaiha
(diamond ocean wave)

Mark ⅜in (1cm) grid, 8 x 8 squares. Mark the diagonal pattern lines. Stitch 288 in white, then stitch lines in rainbow order, starting with pink and stranding across the back as required.

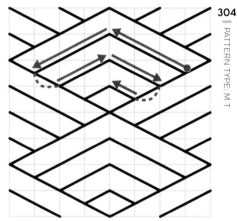

304

PATTERN TYPE: M T

hishi matsuba
(diamond with pine bark diamond)

Mark ⅜in (1cm) grid, 8 x 8 squares. Mark the diagonal pattern lines. Stitch pattern 288 in white. Stitch vertical lines in pink. Stitch remaining lines in rainbow order, stranding across the back as required.

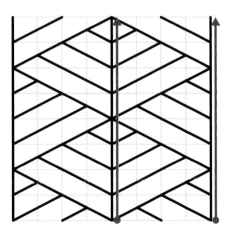

305

PATTERN TYPE: M T

Zigzags

These striking designs are all based around zigzags. The first three patterns are easy to mark, although the others are a little more challenging, but the stitching is quick and easy.

306

PATTERN TYPE: M T

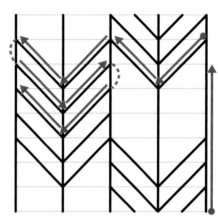

aya sugi
(cedar twill)

Mark ⅜in x ¾in (1cm x 2cm) grid, 8 x 4 rectangles. Mark the diagonal pattern lines. Stitch vertical lines in pink, then continue to stitch zigzags in rainbow order, stranding across the back as required.

307

PATTERN TYPE: M T

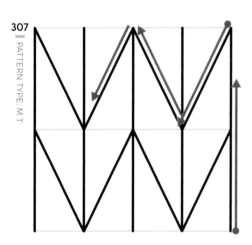

yabane
(arrow feather)

Mark 1½in x ¾in (4cm x 2cm) grid, 2 x 4 rectangles. Mark the diagonal pattern lines. Stitch lines in rainbow order, vertical lines first, then zigzag lines across.

308

PATTERN TYPE: M T

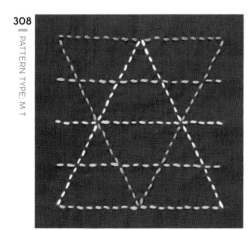
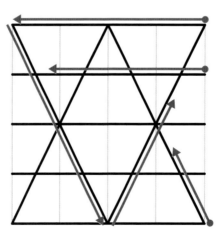

sankaku
(triangles)

Mark ¾in grid (2cm), 4 x 4 squares. Mark the diagonal pattern lines. Stitch lines in rainbow order, horizontal lines first, then the V-shapes. (Alternatively, stitch as two overlapping triangles and three horizontal lines.)

Cedar has a special significance in the Shinto religion. The tall trees are often found at shrines and semamori *(lucky charms) are made from the wood. The arrow is a protective emblem too, with* hamaya *(killing devil arrows) sold at shrines at New Year. The* sankaku *(triangles) design is from a sashiko jacket from Sakata City.*

tsuzuki yamagata
(continued mountain form)

Mark ⅜in (1cm) grid, 8 x 8 squares. Mark the diagonal pattern lines as shown. Stitch pink W-shape, then peach, and continue to stitch remaining zigzags in rainbow order.

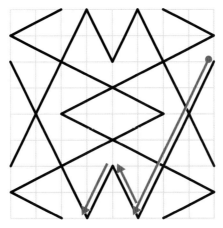

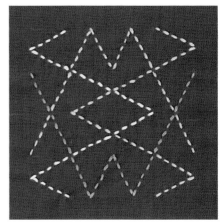

kawari yamaji
(mountain road variation)

Mark ½in (1.3cm) grid, 5 x 5 squares, plus additional line ¼in (6mm) all round. Mark the diagonal pattern lines. Stitch zigzag lines in pink, and continue in rainbow order.

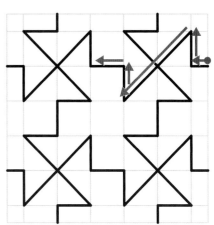

bara moyō tsunagi
(linked rose pattern)

Mark ⅜in grid (1cm), 10 x 10 squares. Mark the diagonal pattern lines. Stitch central crossed lines in pink and peach, then continue to stitch V-shapes and lines individually in rainbow order.

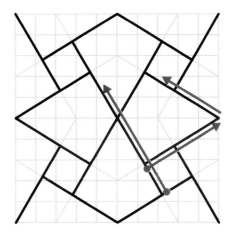

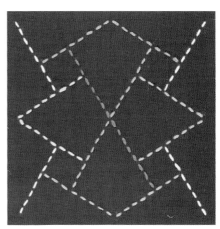

Brocade Patterns

Sayagata brocades were very expensive fabrics, and several variations were aspirational designs for sashiko. Diagonal variations and changing the scale create a different look.

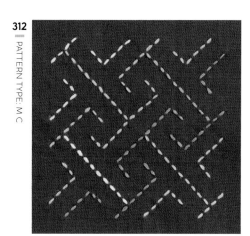
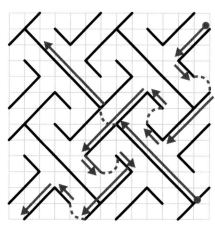

kōji kuzushi
(simple I-form)

Mark ¼in (6mm) grid, 13 x 13 squares. Mark the diagonal pattern lines. Stitch pink line first, stranding across the back as required, then continue in rainbow order.

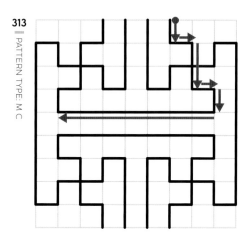
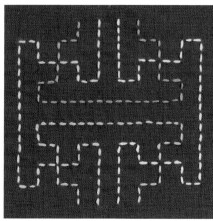

sayagata
(saya pattern)

Mark ⅜in (1cm) grid, 9 x 9 squares. Stitch along first line in pink, then stitch the remaining lines in rainbow order, stepping around the pattern.

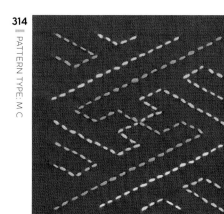
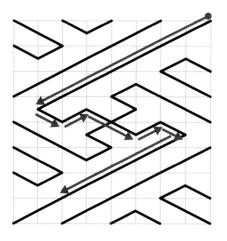

hishi sayagata
(diamond saya pattern)

Mark ⅜in (1cm) grid, 8 x 8 squares. Mark the diagonal pattern lines, lining up your ruler with the grid. Stitch first line in pink, then stitch the remaining lines in rainbow order.

Kuzushi refers to the 'I' shape in the pattern, the kanji character for artisan, manufacture or work. The saya brocade pattern is thought to have travelled east along the Silk Road from the Middle East, arriving in Japan during the Muromachi era (1338–1568CE). It is considered a very high class pattern.

hishi sayagata
(diamond saya pattern)

Mark ¼in (6mm) grid, 12 x 12 squares. Mark the diagonal pattern lines as shown, lining up your ruler with the grid. Stitch first line in pink, then stitch the remaining lines in rainbow order.

kawari sayagata
(saya pattern variation)

Mark ⅜in (1cm) grid, 8 x 8 squares. Mark the diagonal pattern lines as shown. Stitch first line in pink, then stitch the remaining lines in rainbow order.

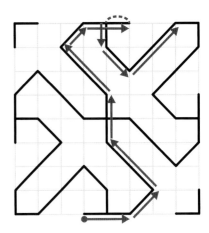

kawari sayagata
(saya pattern variation)

Mark ⅜in (1cm) grid, 8 x 8 squares. Mark the diagonal pattern lines as shown. Stitch first line in pink, then stitch the second line in peach.

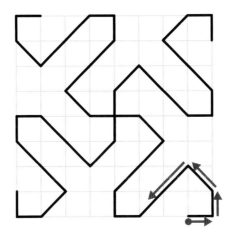
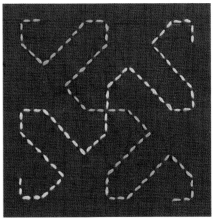

Hemp Leaf

Asanoha (hemp leaf) is one of the most well-known sashiko patterns. The many variations on the six pointed star design can all be drawn on a rectangular grid.

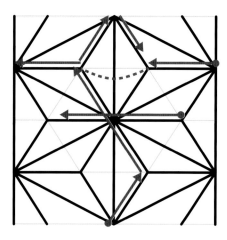

asanoha tsunagi
(linked hemp leaf)

Mark pattern 285. Mark the additional diagonal pattern lines. Note: shallow zigzag blue grid lines go from centre top to fourth line down outside edge and from centre bottom to the fourth line up. Stitch pattern 285 in white. Stitch remaining lines in rainbow order, stranding across the back as required. Horizontal lines can be added at the top and bottom of the design if you wish (not shown).

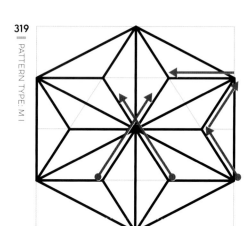

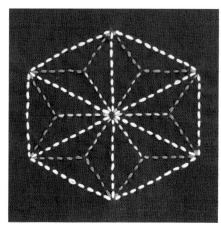

asanoha
(hemp leaf)

Mark pattern 318. Mark the diagonal pattern lines. Stitch pattern 288 in white, and the additional vertical lines to each side. Stitch star outline first in pink, then stitch lines across centre in rainbow order

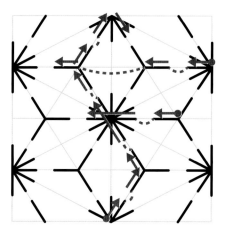

kuzure asanoha
(fragmented hemp leaf)

Mark pattern 318. Stitch the same way as pattern 318, but only stitch the first two and last two stitches of each section of each line, so the pattern seems to disappear.

The asanoha *pattern is believed to bestow good health and long life, making it popular for children's items in particular, and it's found everywhere in Japan and on just about everything! The triangle motif provides protection against evil, so* asanoha *(which combine triangles with diamonds) conveys both strength and beauty.*

tsuno asanoha
(horned hemp leaf)

Mark pattern 318, slightly extending the diagonal lines where they cross. Stitch the same way as pattern 318, crossing the corners by one stitch and stranding across the back as shown.

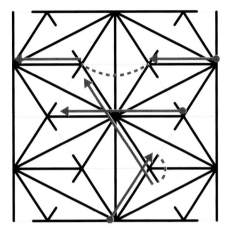
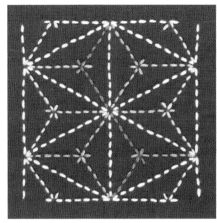

nagai asanoha
(elongated hemp leaf)

Mark ¾in (2cm) grid, 4 x 4 squares. Mark the diagonal pattern lines. Stitch three vertical lines in white, then stitch two vertical lines in pink, continuing stitching in rainbow order. The stitch sequence is as pattern 318 (note: diagram arrows omitted for clarity).

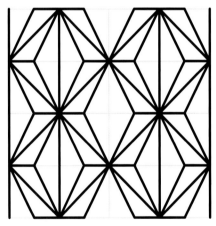

kawari asanoha
(hemp leaf variation)

Mark pattern 318. Mark short additional lines approx. ⅛in (3mm) from pattern lines. Stitch pattern 318 in white. Stitch short lines in rainbow order as shown, two stitches in each, continuing in white.

Star and Hexagon

This series of patterns was inspired by an old *katazome* stencil pattern and are similar to *asanoha* (hemp leaf). They are all drawn on the same basic grid.

324

PATTERN TYPE: M C

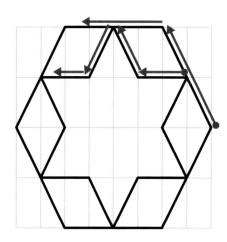

hoshi kikkō
(star hexagon)

Mark ¾in x ⅜in (2cm x 1cm) grid, 4 x 8 rectangles. Mark the diagonal pattern lines. Stitch hexagon outline in pink. Stitch star in peach.

325

PATTERN TYPE: M C

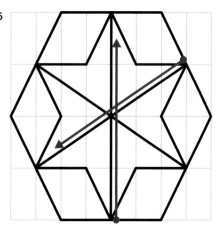

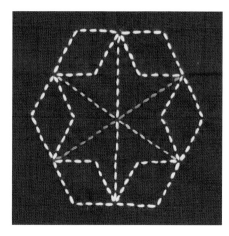

kawari hoshi kikkō
(star hexagon variation)

Mark pattern 324. Mark the additonal diagonal and vertical pattern lines crossing through the centre of the star as shown. Stitch pattern 324 in white. Stitch diagonal lines individually in pink and peach, and the vertical line in yellow.

326

PATTERN TYPE: M C

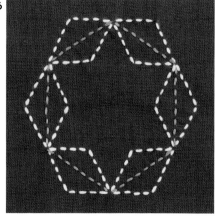

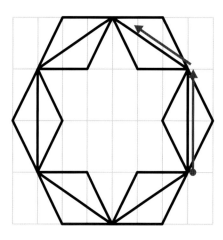

kawari hoshi kikkō
(star hexagon variation)

Mark pattern 324. Mark the additonal diagonal pattern lines as shown to make the inner hexagon. Stitch pattern 324 in white. Stitch inner hexagon outline in pink.

Katazome stench-dyed fabrics were developed during the Edo era (1603 –1868CE), as way to dye patterned fabrics more economically. The stencils were made from layers of tough mulberry paper treated with persimmon tannin, and any delicate parts of the pattern were reinforced with a fine mesh of human hair.

kawari hoshi kikkō
(star hexagon variation)

Mark pattern 324. Mark the additional diagonal pattern lines in the corners. Stitch hexagon outline in pink. Stitch remaining lines in rainbow order.

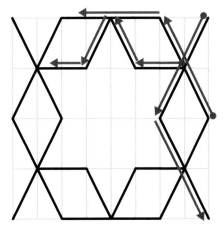 

kawari asanoha
(hemp leaf variation)

Mark pattern 327. Use a 3in (8cm) circle template to draw the shallow arcs. Stitch hexagon outline and side diamonds in white. Stitch curves and remaining lines in rainbow order.

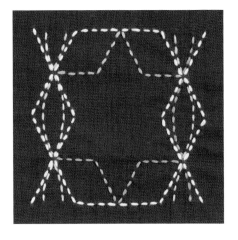 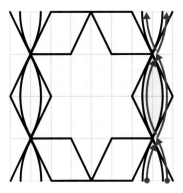

kawari hoshi kikkō
(star hexagon variation)

Mark pattern 327. Mark the additonal diagonal pattern lines crossing through the centre as shown. Stitch pattern 327 in white, then stitch diagonal lines as pattern 325, in pink.

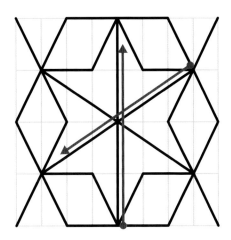 

Hemp Leaf and Diamonds

More patterns linking hemp leaf and diamond motifs with different infills, including *kuzure asanoha* (fragmented hemp leaf). Hemp leaf fits into a six pointed star, so is often interspersed with diamonds or hexagons.

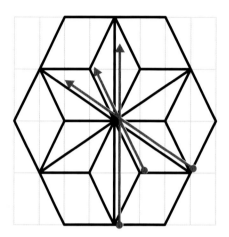

asanoha to hishi
(hemp leaf and diamond)

Mark pattern 324. Mark additional diagonal lines crossing through the centre as shown. Stitch pattern 324 in white, then stitch diagonal lines in rainbow order.

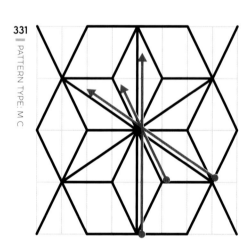
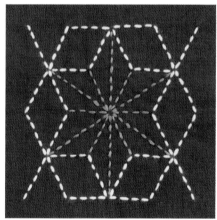

tsunagi asanoha to hishi
(linked hemp leaf and diamond)

Mark pattern 333. Mark additional diagonal pattern lines crossing through the centre as shown. Stitch pattern 327 in white. Stitch diagonal lines in pink.

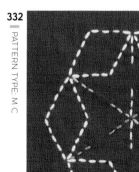
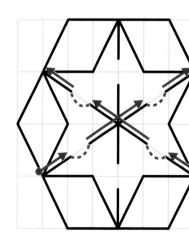

kuzure asanoha to hishi
(fragmented hemp leaf and diamond)

Mark pattern 324. Mark additional diagonal lines crossing through the centre as shown. Stitch 324 in white. Stitch diagonal lines individually, stitching the first and last two stitches of each section only.

tsunagi kuzure asanoha to hishi
(linked fragmented hemp leaf and diamond)

Mark pattern 327. Mark additional diagonal lines crossing through the centre as shown. Stitch pattern 327 in white, then stitch diagonal lines individually, as pattern 332, in pink.

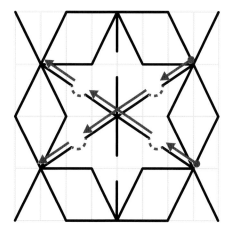 

333
PATTERN TYPE: M C

kawari asanoha to hishi
(hemp leaf and diamond variation)

Mark pattern 330. Mark a ¾in (2cm) circle in the centre. Stitch as pattern 330, but stitch diagonal lines with just two stitches in and out of the centre, in rainbow order.

 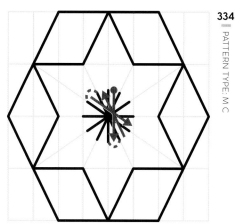

334
PATTERN TYPE: M C

tsunagi asanoha to hishi
(linked hemp leaf and diamond)

Mark pattern 327 and the centre of pattern 334. Mark shallow arcs using a 1½in (4cm) circle template. Stitch pattern 327 in white. Stitch centre of pattern 334 in pink. Stitch remaining lines in rainbow order.

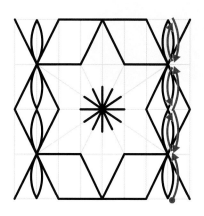 

335
PATTERN TYPE: M C

Hemp Leaf Variations

Asanoha (hemp leaf) has several variations with twisted, bent, curved or zigzagged lines, or tiny stars. These are tricky to mark, but worth it!

336

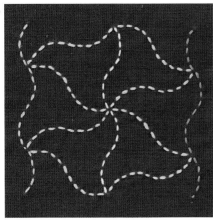

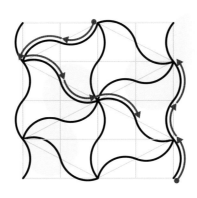

chidori tsunagi
(linked plovers)

Mark pattern 285 on a ¾in (2cm) grid, 4 x 4 squares. Use a 1⅛in (3cm) circle template to mark wavy lines, changing curve direction half way along each line. Stitch in the same order as pattern 285.

337

nejire asanoha
(twisted hemp leaf)

Mark pattern 318, and then mark pattern 336 on top. Mark a single curve on all the shallow zigzag and horizontal lines. Stitch in same order as pattern 318.

338

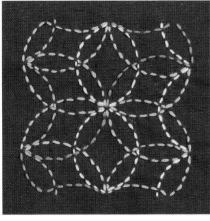

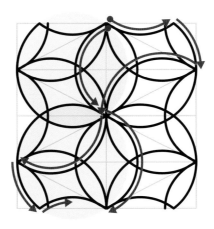

hanazashi
(flower stitch)

Mark pattern 318 as a guideline. Mark pattern with overlapping 2in (5cm) circles and ovals, making a thin card oval template. Stitch diagonal wavy lines, starting with pink and continuing in rainbow order.

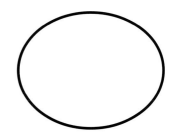

Asanoha is such a popular pattern that inevitably many variations have evolved. Hanazashi and gizagiza asanoha are two such adaptations, appearing in Hokusai's 1824 book Shingata Komoncho (New Forms of Small Patterns). It's not known if he invented the designs included or collated those in fashion – perhaps it's both.

rokkaku kamon
(hexagon pattern)

Mark pattern 318 with 'stars' on top. Mark the additional diagonal lines approx. ¾in (2cm) long for each 'star'. Stitch stars individually crossing over lines, with the central star stitched in pink and peach. Note: the stitches in the stars are longer than the white stitches. Complete stars in rainbow order. Stitch pattern 318 in white, stopping and starting lines at the stars, stranding thread across the back behind them.

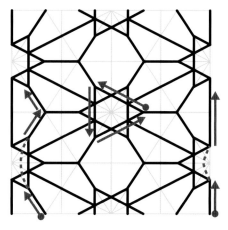 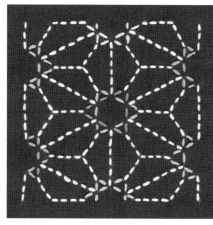

kawari asanoha
(hemp leaf variation)

Mark pattern 285. Mark shapes within triangles, with points ⅛in (3mm) from corners and the bend ¼in (6mm) in from the triangles' sides. Stitch pattern 285 in white. Stitch bent lines in rainbow order, stranding across the back as required.

 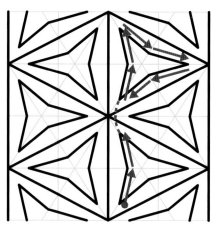

gizagiza asanoha
(jagged asanoha)

Mark pattern 318 as a guideline. Mark a skinny zigzag over each line, with the Z-bend in the same direction, using thin card zigzag templates. The stitch sequence is as pattern 318 (note: diagram arrows omitted for clarity).

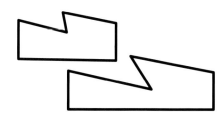

Buddhist Designs

Manji, the Buddhist symbol for harmony and good luck, has already appeared in several patterns. Here are more designs with links to Buddhism, including *ryūsō kikkō* as dragons are always present as temple guardians.

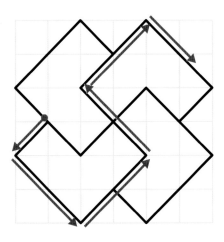

manji
(Buddhist symbol)

Mark ½in (1.3cm) grid, 6 x 6 squares. Mark the diagonal pattern lines as shown. Stitch with pink and peach crossed lines.

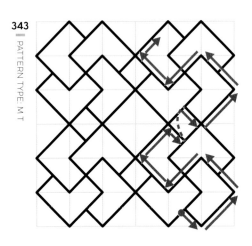

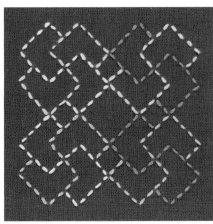

manji tsunagi
(linked Buddhist symbol)

Mark ½in (1.3cm) grid, 6 x 6 squares. Mark diagonal pattern lines as shown. Stitch the pink line first, stranding across the back as required, then continue in rainbow order.

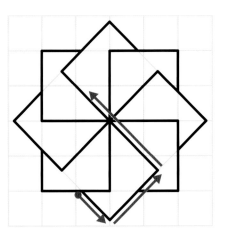

ishiguruma
(stone wheel)

Mark ½in (1.3cm) grid, 6 x 6 squares. Mark diagonal pattern lines as shown. Note: the diagonal squares are 1in (2.5cm) square. Stitch in rainbow order.

The manji *is a left facing hooked cross, and it is often seen on the chest, feet or palms of statues of the Buddha. It is used to represent all of creation, and the word literally means 'ten thousand', aka 'eternity'. It is synonymous with the dharma wheel, which symbolises cosmic law and order.*

tokosho tsunagi
(linked tokosho crosses)

Mark ⅜in (1cm) grid, 8 x 8 squares. Mark the diagonal pattern lines and crosses on the grid as shown, so each side is ⅜in (1cm). Stitch crosses individually. Stitch diagonals, stranding across the back of the central cross as shown.

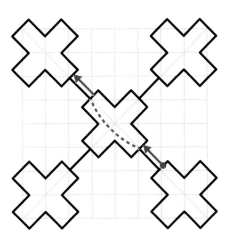
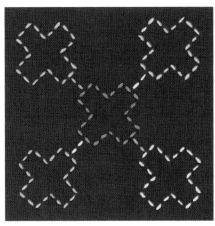

mitsuba
(Japanese wild parsley)

Mark 3½in (9cm) square with ¼in (6mm) horizontal lines and vertical lines ½in (1.3cm) from each side and in the centre. Mark overlapping 2in (5cm) circles. Stitch each motif individually in rainbow order.

ryūsō kikkō
(dragon claw hexagon)

Mark ⅜in (1cm) grid, 8 x 8 squares. Mark pattern 285. Mark additional diagonal lines in each triangle as shown, lining up the ends with the grid. Stitch pattern 285 in white. Stitch remaining lines in rainbow order.

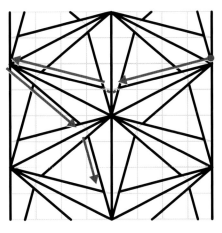
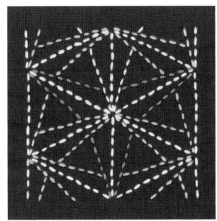

Kanji Characters

The kanji characters for the seasons are a good choice for a year long stitching project. *Fuji san* (Mount Fuji) and *mitsu tomoe* (triple comma) are both *kamon*, Japanese family crests.

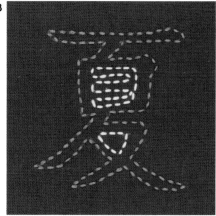

haru
(spring)

Trace off the motif (see Techniques) from the actual size pattern. Stitch around the kanji outline in pink, then fill in the central sections in white.

natsu
(summer)

Trace off the motif (see Techniques) from the actual size pattern. Stitch around the kanji outline in green, then fill in the central sections in blue.

aki
(autumn)

Trace off the motif (see Techniques) from the actual size pattern. Stitch around the kanji outlines in yellow and peach, stranding across to the short dashes on the right hand radical.

Japanese kanji are derived from Chinese characters, with thousands of combinations of radicals (i.e. the basic kanji). With the katakana and hiragana syllabaries, they make an elegant if complex writing system.

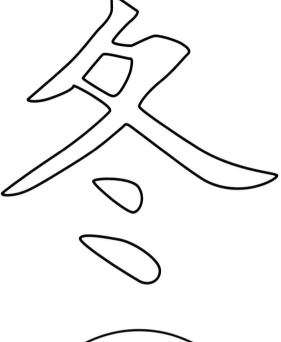

fūyō
(winter)

Trace off the motif (see Techniques) from the actual size pattern. Stitch around the kanji outlines in white and lilac, stranding across to the short dashes under the main kanji outline.

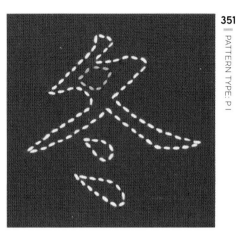

351

mitsu tomoe
(triple comma)

Trace off the motif (see Techniques) from the actual size pattern. Stitch each comma individually in pink, peach, and yellow, starting and finishing at the point.

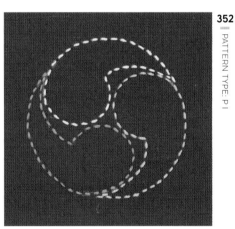

352

fuji san
(Mount Fuji)

Trace off the motif (see Techniques) from the actual size pattern. Stitch the mist in lilac, then stitch Mount Fuji in pink and white.

353

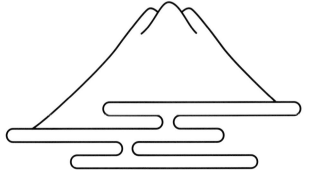

Seasonal Motifs

In Japan, flowers and leaves are strongly associated with the seasons in which they bloom. Choose natural thread colours or continue your colour theme to suit the motifs.

354

ume
(plum blossom)

Trace off the motif (see Techniques) from the actual size pattern. Stitch around the petals in pink, then stitch the centre in yellow, stranding across the back as required.

355

sakura
(cherry blossom)

Trace off the motif (see Techniques) from the actual size pattern. Stitch around the petals in pink, then stitch the centre in yellow, stranding across the back as required.

356

take
(bamboo)

Trace off the motif (see Techniques) from the actual size pattern. Stitch around the leaves in green, then stitch the veins in white, stranding across the back as required.

132

Items decorated with individual seasonal flowers or groupings are used only in that season, or slightly ahead of it. Combining them all together means an item can be used year round.

kikkyo
(Chinese bellflower)

Trace off the motif (see Techniques) from the actual size pattern. Stitch around the flower in lilac, then stitch the inner lines in white, stranding across the back as required.

kikku
(chrysanthemum)

Trace off the motif (see Techniques) from the actual size pattern. Stitch around the centre in yellow, then stitch the petals in white, stranding across the back as required.

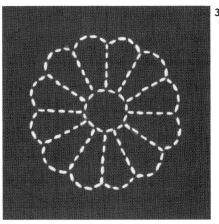

momiji
(maple leaf)

Trace off the motif (see Techniques) from the actual size pattern. Stitch the leaf outline in peach, then stitch the veins in green.

Kamon Crests

Kamon (Japanese family crests) may be used decoratively as well as by a particular family, and they include geometric designs, objects, natural phenomena, in addition to flora and fauna.

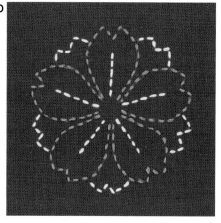

360

kasane sakura
(layered cherry blossom)

Trace off the motif (see Techniques) from the actual size pattern. Stitch the whole petals in pink, then stitch the outer petals in white, stranding across the back as required.

361

takenoko
(bamboo shoot)

Trace off the motif (see Techniques) from the actual size pattern. Stitch the leaf outlines in green, the veins and shoots in yellow, stranding across the back as required. Stitch the snowball semicircle in white.

362

tachibana
(orange blossom)

Trace off the motif (see Techniques) from the actual size pattern. Stitch the flower shape in white, then stitch the leaves and stems in green, yellow and peach, stranding across the back as required.

134

Kamon originated over a thousand years ago, and were originally used by the aristocracy and the samurai class, before spreading to commoners during the seventeenth century.

tsuki
(moon)

Trace off the motif (see Techniques) from the actual size pattern. Stitch the moon in white and the clouds in lilac, stranding across the back as required.

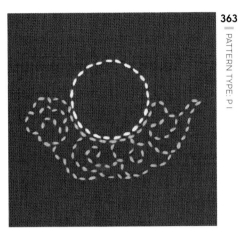

mitsu yabane
(three arrows)

Trace off the motif (see Techniques) from the actual size pattern. Stitch the circle centre and the arrow shafts in yellow, then stitch the feathers in white, stranding across the back as required.

sensu
(fan)

Trace off the motif (see Techniques) from the actual size pattern. Stitch the fan sticks in yellow and the fan paper outline in pink. Stitch the fan folds in peach, stranding across the back as required.

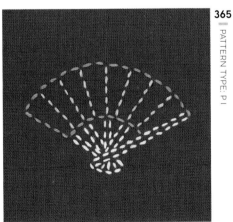

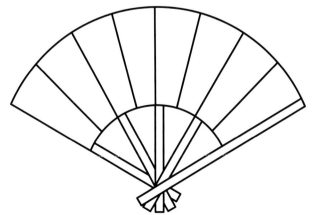

Making the Quilt

This stunning quilt measures approximately 96in (244cm) square, and is a easy design with narrow sashing strips and small cornerstones linking the sashiko blocks. Choose fabrics to complement your sashiko thread colours, with long border strips in a another complementary fabric. It is simply quilted 'in the ditch' along each strip of blocks, which may be done by hand or machine. Of course, you may use your sashiko blocks for other projects but combining them in this sampler quilt makes a wonderful record of your sashiko journey.

YOU WILL NEED

+ 365 sashiko blocks, each 4½in (11.5cm) square

+ 3.5yd (3.25m) of plain cotton fabric, 42in (107cm) wide, for sashing and narrow borders, cut as follows:*

    + 684 strips for sashiko block sashing, each 4½ x 1in (11.5 x 2.5cm)

    + 4 strips 4½ x 1in (11.5 x 1in) and 12 strips 5 x 1in (12.7 x 1cm), for border sashiko blocks

    + 8 strips for narrow borders, each 85½ x 1in (217 x 2.5cm)

+ 4 fabric strips for wide borders, each 85½ x 4½in (217 x 11.5cm)

+ 328 cornerstone squares, each 1in (2.5cm)**

+ Cotton fabric for backing, 98in (249cm) square***

+ Wadding (batting), 98in (249cm) square

+ 10¾yd (9.75m) of 1¾in (4.5cm) bias binding****

+ No. 50 cotton sewing thread, to match main fabric colour, approx. 330yd (300m)

+ Hand or machine quilting threads to match main fabric colours, approx. 165yd (150m)

*More is needed if using an ombré shaded fabric, which requires fussy cutting to create the shaded effect on the quilt (see Cutting the Sashing Strips). Note: the long, narrow border strips may be pieced from strips cut across the fabric width.

** The cornerstones can be cut from fabric scraps, but if cutting from a single piece of fabric, exactly 10in (25.4cm) of 42in (107cm) wide fabric is required.

*** The backing fabric can be pieced from narrower fabric: avoid positioning piecing seams along the middle of the quilt and use a ⅜in (1cm) seam allowance; press seams open to reduce bulk.

**** To make your own bias binding to match the sashing fabric, allow for an extra 1yd (1m) of fabric: cut diagonal 1¾in (4.5cm) strips; join into one continuous strip with ¼in (6mm) diagonal seams, pressed open; press strip in half lengthwise. If using ombré shaded fabric, use sashing strip leftovers: for exact shading alignment, cut across the fabric width and piece strip to match the narrow border colours.

Finished size of patchwork: 95½in (243cm) square (this may be slightly smaller due to the number of patchwork seams, and a little smaller after quilting)

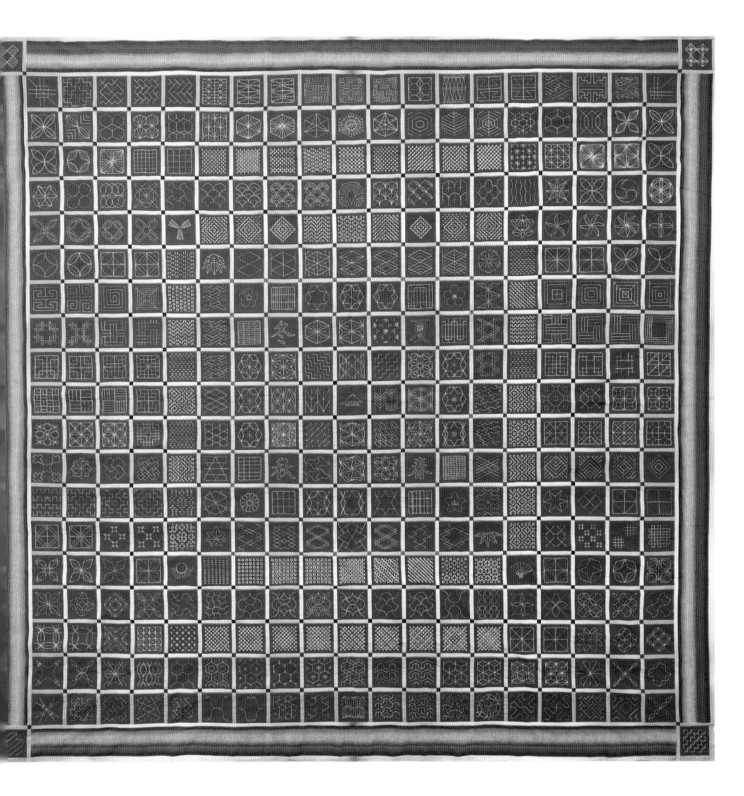

For my finished sampler patchwork, I put directional designs (like kanji characters, kamon crests, or clamshell patterns, with an obvious right way up) in the centre, keeping non directional patterns in four outer columns on each side, to hang down the sides of my bed. Blocks with strong diagonal elements are in cornerstone positions outwards from the centre. The dense hitomezashi (one stitch sashiko) are arranged in borders, with other patterns arranged in rows, columns or groups with visually similar patterns, not always the same as the Pattern Directory groups. Play with your sashiko blocks for your favourite arrangement.

CUTTING THE SASHING STRIPS

Cut 1in (2.5cm) strips across the width of the folded 42in (107cm) wide sashing fabric. Check that you are cutting exactly at right angles to the fold; cut the folded strip into strips 4½in (11.5cm) long. This makes nine sashing strips, with one strip cut across the central fold and pressed open. Two strips make eighteen sashing strip – you will need nineteen per patchwork row, so cut the extras separately. If you are using ombré shaded fabric, read my tips below, and sort the cut strips into groups by colour (see Assemble the quilt top, step 2).

If you are using an ombré shaded fabric that shades to the centre and back again, so the selvedges are identical in colour, you need 3¾yd (3.5m) to be absolutely sure to match the colour shading. The extra forty central sashing pieces can be cut from either side of the fabric **(A)**, twenty from each side. The narrow border strips are cut from the same fabric; these need to be joined in the middle to continue the shading. The leftover fabric can be used for the quilt binding, if you wish, or included in a pieced backing panel.

If you are using an ombré shaded fabric that shades from one side to the other, so the selvedges are different colours (like mine), the extra forty sashing pieces needed to continue the colour shading across the centre of each sashing row can only be cut from one selvedge side **(B)**. This means extra fabric, so allow 4½yd (4m).

The way you arrange cutting the strips from ombré fabric will vary depending on its colour shading. For example, you may find that one side of the colour shade has a tiny touch of a bright colour that you don't want to use, or there may be a wider area of colour shading at one side, so look at how your fabric shades and adjust how close you cut to the selvedge.

CHECKING YOUR SEAM ALLOWANCE

Use ¼in (6mm) seams throughout. Stitch a few test pieces to check your seam allowance is accurate. If machine sewing, use a ¼in (6mm) presser foot, or adjust the needle position for a ¼in (6mm) seam. If hand sewing, use a fabric marker to mark ¼in (6mm) along either side of each strip **(C)** as stitching guidelines.

Note: stitch handsewn seams with small running stitches approx. ¹⁄₁₆in (1.5mm) with an occasional back stitch; start and finish with a knot and a few back stitches. Always pin seams at right angles to the stitching line. If machine stitching, remove each pin before it goes under the needle.

Assemble the quilt top

1. Organise the sashiko blocks into your preferred arrangement, pinning them to a large bed sheet or design wall at least 86in (2.17m) square. There are many options:

✦ In numerical order in columns (vertically) or rows (horizontally); columns can start on the left, or the right (like Japanese writing!); rows can go from side to side, or back and forth.

✦ In numerical order, spiralling outwards from a first central block; like the first option, this also gives a sense of stitching progression.

✦ Symmetrically, starting with a single central block and matching up similar blocks on opposite sides in each round: mirror image or rotational, your choice.

Make a simple paper plan and number each block lightly on the back to indicate the position of each in your chosen arrangement (numbered to 1 to 365, to include the four corner blocks!).

2. Unpin each block in turn to check it is facing the right way up before sewing on the sashing onto the right-hand edge, right sides together **(D)**. Press the seam towards the sashing. Note: if the seam allowance

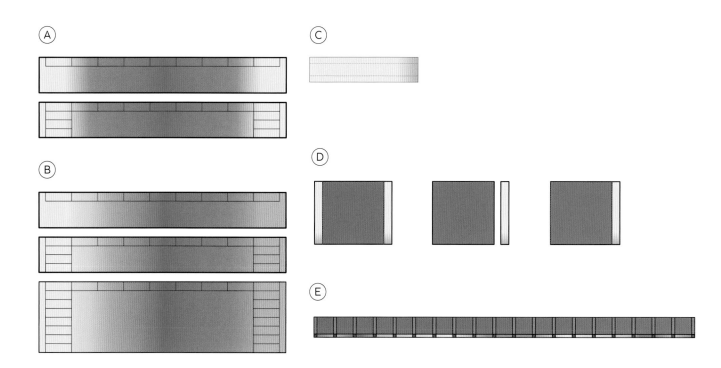

is correct, once blocks are joined by the sashing and seams pressed, the block edges will touch behind the narrow sashing strips. If you are using an ombré fabric, take care that the attached strip follows the colour progression and that the strip shading runs in the right direction. Return the block to the design wall before unpinning the next one.

3. Once the sashing is attached to the blocks, sew the first horizontal row of nineteen blocks together, pressing seams towards the sashing. Now sew nineteen horizontal sashing strips together into one long strip with eighteen 1in (2.5cm) cornerstone squares in between **(E)**, again pressing the seams towards the sashing. Pin the cornerstone sashing strip to the bottom edge of the sashiko block strip, lining up the vertical sashing pieces with the cornerstone squares, nestling the seam allowances together snugly. Pin, then sew. Repeat to sew a cornerstone sashing strip to the bottom edge of each row of sashiko blocks, except the final row of sashiko blocks.

4. Join the horizontal sections together in pairs, pressing towards the sashing strips each time. Sew each pair together making groups of four, until all the sections are joined. With nineteen horizontal sections, there will be one group of three **(F)**.

5. Measure your patchwork through the centre before adding the borders and the corner blocks. With so many seams, it is likely that the quilt centre now measures slightly less than the border strips, so trim the borders to fit. Sew a narrow 1in (2.5cm) border strip to either side of each wide 4½in (11.5cm) border strip. Press seams towards the narrow border strips.

6. Now sew the border strips to the four remaining sashiko blocks to form the corners of the quilt border **(G)**. Press the seam of the cornerstone square towards the sashing, and press the other sashing seams away from the sashiko block.

7. Sew the prepared corner block to each end of the side borders, as also seen in **(G)**.

Press seams towards the border pieces. Pin and sew the top and bottom border strips to the quilt centre, folding each to find the quarter points, marking with pins. Match up the quarter points first and pin, then match and pin the ends, then the rest of the strip, and sew. Press seams towards the borders. Pin, sew and press the side border strips in the same way. Press towards the outside of the quilt top.

The quilt sandwich

8. Press the quilt top and the backing fabric. Lay the backing right side down on a flat surface, using masking tape to hold larger panels in place, with the wadding (batting) on top and smoothed out, then place the quilt top on top. Measure diagonally across the quilt in both directions to check that the quilt top is square.

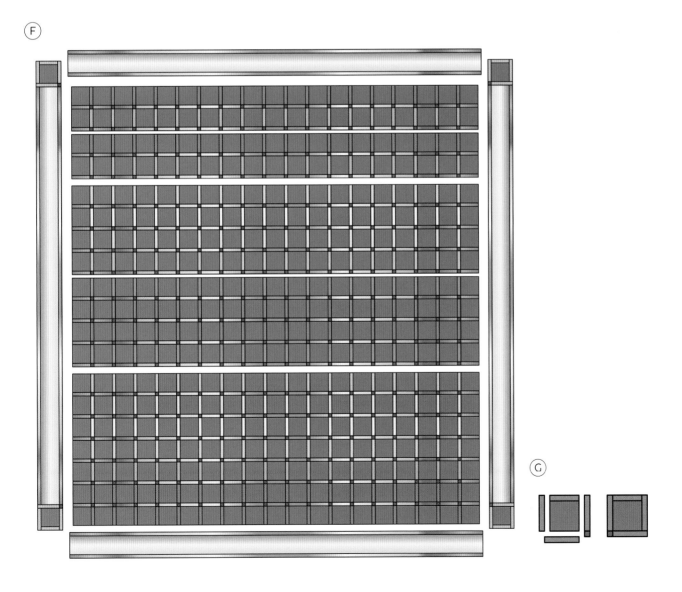

(F)

(G)

9. Thread tack (baste) the three layers of your quilt sandwich together (less risky than pins which might snag your sashiko stitching), alternating large and small running stitches radiating from the centre outwards or along each sashing strip. Many long arm quilters offer a tacking (basting) service if this is too daunting!

Quilting and binding

10. Quilt up and down and from side to side in a grid pattern, 'in the ditch' between sashiko block and sashing strip. If hand quilting, you may skip each cornerstone and recommence at the corner of the next sashiko block. If machine quilting, use a walking foot to sew in straight lines across the sashing and cornerstones. The border may be left unquilted, or have a simple design, such as a few parallel lines. Once quilting is complete, sew about ⅛in (3mm) from the edge all the way around, then trim wadding and backing to the quilt top edge.

11. Pin the raw edges of the binding strip to the bottom edge of the top of the quilt, lining it up with the quilt edge. Start approx. 10in (25cm) from the end of the binding strip with a few backstitches and sew the

binding to the quilt by machine or by hand, stitching approx. ¼in (6mm) from the edge, to ensure a snug fit when folded over. Note: if hand sewing the binding in running stitch, make sure to stitch through all layers and do a backstitch every few stitches. As you approach the end of the first side, stop stitching approx. ¼in (6mm) from the edge with a few backstitches **(H)**.

12. Fold back the binding strip at 45° and pin, forming the mitre **(I)**. Fold the strip back down to continue sewing the binding to the quilt **(J)**. Repeat at each corner.

13. Open out the start of the binding and cut on a 45° angle, refold and pin along the quilt edge. Pin the other end of the binding along the last side of the quilt. Where the binding meets together, trim this other end on a 45° angle to match the slope at the start of the binding strip, adding a ½in (1.3cm) seam allowance to the end, overlapping the ends and sewing together with a ¼in (6mm) seam **(K)**. Press seam open. Finish sewing the binding along the side of the quilt.

14. Turn the quilt over to hemstitch the folded edge of the binding to the back **(L and M)**. The mitres will fall easily into place as you fold the binding around the corners.

Block 366: the label

15. For your bonus leap year sashiko block, make a quilt label. Write your text (date of completion, your name, etc.) onto a 4½in (11.5cm) sashiko fabric square – I used a lettering stencil! Note: capital letters tend to be to be easier to stitch than lower case. Once the stitching is complete, press under ¼in (6mm) all round the finished block and hand sew it to the back of your quilt. Your Sashiko 365 sampler quilt is complete. Congratulations and thank you for sharing this journey!

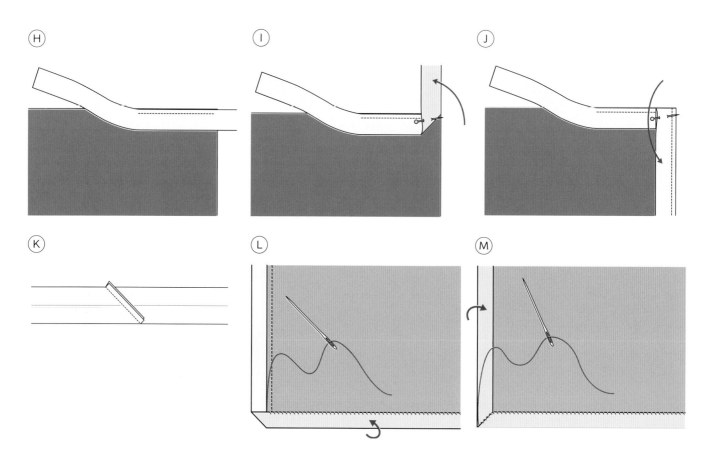

Mark Up Grids

Grid Pattern 1 is divided into ½in, ¼in and ⅛in (1.3cm, 6mm and 3mm) increments, with the ½in (1.3cm) and ¼in (6mm) lines in a heavier line weight; Grid Pattern 2 is divided into ⅜in and ⅛in (1cm and 3mm) increments, with the ⅜in (1cm) lines in a heavier weight. The small arrows indicate the midpoint of each side. You can use these to mark your blocks in exactly the same way as the lines on a cutting mat. If you don't want to draw on the book, you may photocopy these grids for your own use.

You can cut out this page for easy reference. Remember to keep it somewhere safe!

GRID 1: For drawing ½in grid

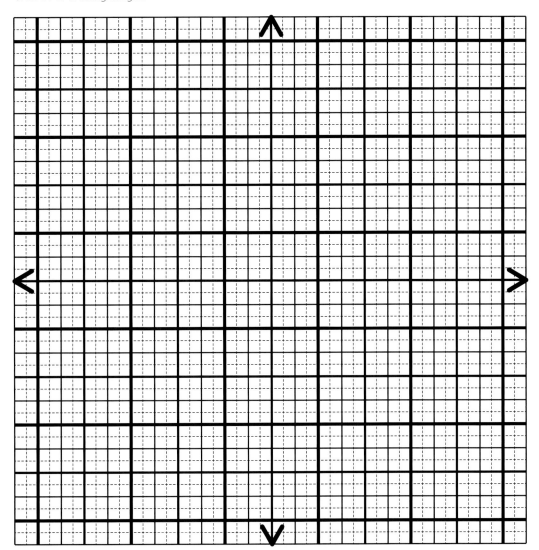

GRID 2: For drawing ⅜in grid

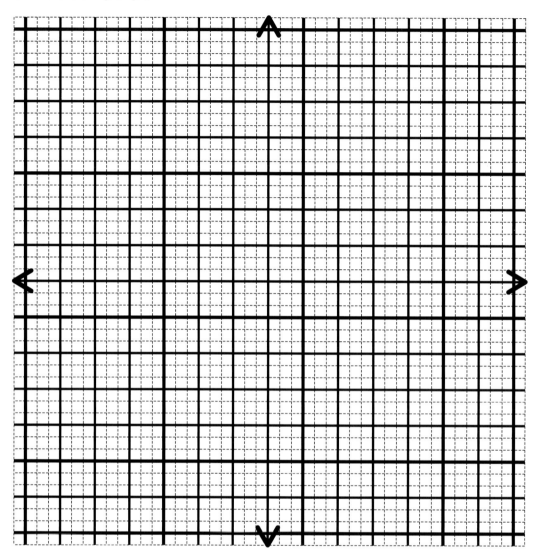

Suppliers

Susan Briscoe Designs (UK)

www.susanbriscoe.com

The Crafty Quilter (UK)

www.craftyquilter.co.uk

Japan Crafts (UK)

www.japancrafts.co.uk

Marita Rolin (Sweden)

www.maritarolin.se

BeBe Bold Europe (France)

bebebold.eu

BeBe Bold (Australia)

www.bebebold.com

Indigo Niche (Australia)

www.indigoniche.com

Wabi-Sabi Designs (Australia)

wabi-sabi.com.au

Kimonomomo (USA)

www.kimonomomo.etsy.com

Shibori Dragon (USA)

www.shiboridragon.com

Upcycle Stitches (USA)

upcyclestitches.com

A Threaded Needle (Canada)

www.athreadedneedle.com

Yuzawaya (Japan)

www.yuzawaya.co.jp

Acknowledgements

I would like to thank the following people for their help in planning and creating this sashiko book – my sashiko teachers and friends at Yuza Sashiko Guild; all the team at David and Charles publishers, who have created this beautiful book from my text and stitching; Olympus Thread Mfg. Co. (Japan); my husband Glyn for his support; and the students who have attended my sashiko workshops over the last two decades.

About the Author

Susan Briscoe is a leading expert in the traditional Japanese sewing technique, sashiko. She began stitching sashiko in 2000, on a return visit to the Japanese town where she worked as an assistant English teacher (Yuza-machi, Yamagata Prefecture). Since then, she has studied and researched sashiko, taught sashiko worldwide, organized sashiko exhibitions, and worked closely with Yuza Sashiko Guild, bringing them to the UK to teach many times. She also specialises in kogin, boro, patchwork and quilting, and is the author of over a dozen books on these subjects.

OTHER SASHIKO BOOKS BY SUSAN BRISCOE:

+ The Ultimate Sashiko Sourcebook
+ Japanese Sashiko Inspirations
+ Simple Sashiko

In memory of my dad, who helped me plan the original idea for working with the rainbow in this book. Thank you for giving me your engineer's eye for pattern!

ISBN-13: 9781446309254 paperback
ISBN-13: 9781446381717 EPUB
ISBN-13: 9781446381700 PDF

FSC
www.fsc.org

MIX
Paper | Supporting
responsible forestry
FSC® C020056

Printed in China by Leo Paper Products Ltd for:
David and Charles, Ltd
Suite A, Tourism House, Pynes Hill, Exeter, EX2 5WS

10 9 8 7 6 5

Publishing Director: Ame Verso
Senior Commissioning Editor: Sarah Callard
Managing Editor: Jeni Chown
Editor: Jessica Cropper
Project Editor: Cheryl Brown
Head of Design: Anna Wade
Designer: Sam Staddon
Pre-press Designer: Ali Stark
Illustrations: Kuo Kang Chen
Photography: Jason Jenkins and Chris Grady
Production Manager: Beverley Richardson

David and Charles publishes high-quality books on a wide range of subjects. For more information visit www.davidandcharles.com.

Share your makes with us on social media using #dandcbooks and #sashiko365. Follow us on Facebook and Instagram by searching for @dandcbooks.

Layout of the digital edition of this book may vary depending on reader hardware and display settings.